Organisations and Leadership during Covid-19

Organisations and Leadership during Covid-19

Studies using Systems Leadership Theory

SLT Practioners

McGill, Macdonald, Barnett, Dixon, Highfield, Farrands, Palmer, Chaston & Mitchell

SL DA

Systems Leadership Development Association

CONTENTS

CONTENTS

| viii |

ACKNOWLEDGMENTS

This project was initiated in early 2020 by Geoff McGill about the time the World Health Organisation (WHO) declared Covid-19 as a pandemic. With encouragement and support from Ian Macdonald, the project grew in scope over the course of 2020 and 2021. In all, nine authors have contributed individually or jointly to nine chapters across a diverse range of public and private organisations, including corporations with global operations.

Thanks are due to Mark Potter, Rob Chaston and Geoff McGill who took the book forward to publication and to the Systems Leadership Development Association (SLDA) for its financial and logistical support.

ABOUT THE AUTHORS

Geoff McGill, Ian Macdonald, Hilton Barnett, Clive Dixon, Rob Chaston and Graeme Mitchell are consultants whose work is largely built upon a set of practical and proven concepts known as Systems Leadership Theory. They each operate their own consultancies working in partnership with leaders in organisations to help create positive and productive outcomes and help create the conditions where people can work creatively, knowing they will be treated with respect and fairness. Each of them has worked in organisations at senior levels and have experience in applying and shaping these models so that they work in practice not just theory. These six authors also form part of a network of consultants based around the world known as Macdonald Associates Consultancy, working with a range of organisations across all sectors. More information on their individual biographies can be found at https://www.maconsultancy.com/who-we-are.

Dr Julie Highfield is a Consultant Clinical Psychologist working for the National Health Service in the United Kingdom. She has worked across a number of different medical settings and is currently based in critical care services. She is the Lead for the Critical Care and Major Trauma Psychology service and works as the Organisational Health Consultant to the wider service. She is also the National Wellbeing Director for the Intensive Care Society, leading a national project for the intensive care workforce.

Don Farrands is a QC at the Victorian Bar, a chartered accountant, and a director. He has significant and varied experience in law, commerce, the arts, and community organisations, including in the disability sector. He lives in Melbourne. During Don's time as a senior executive within the Rio Tinto Ltd group, he was introduced to and has since been an exponent of Systems Leadership principles and practices.

Tom Palmer is CEO of Newmont which is the largest gold producer in the world with operations in nine countries. Tom has previously had a very successful career in Rio Tinto including high level leadership roles in aluminium, copper, iron ore and coal. Tom has a globally recognised reputation for his concerns and work in safety and social responsibility and is known for his understanding of the importance of treating all people well and fairly. He has been familiar with Systems Leadership throughout his career and has applied its principles with creativity and imagination in many different situations.

INTRODUCTION

All of us have direct experience of how the Covid-19 Pandemic has affected the world around us, our families, the people with whom we interact and work and the different regions and countries where we live. These experiences are part of a universal shared context. This study concerns a particular aspect of that context – organisational and leadership responses to the Pandemic.

The purpose of this book is to demonstrate how the body of knowledge known as Systems Leadership can be used to better explain why organisational and leadership responses to the Covid-19 Pandemic were effective (or not).

Examples will demonstrate good practice but also help understand why some were less successful.

Many readers will be familiar with Systems Leadership, others may not. So to set context especially for those less familiar this brief summay may help:

Systems Leadership Theory (Systems Leadership: Creating Positive Organisations; Macdonald, Burke and Stewart, Routledge 2018) is a coherent approach to understanding and more importantly predicting how people are likely to behave in different social and organisational contexts. It is based on over 60 years of research and observation of good practice across a wide range of organisations in many different countries.

The authors' intention is to provide a theoretically based but practically applicable set of concepts and tools that enable the creation of organisations that encourage people to use their creativity, express their potential and contribute to a just society.

It integrates what are often considered to be separate subjects such as leadership, teamwork, capability, structure, systems, roles and role relationships, authority and power. It explicitly takes into account the importance of our context and builds on the underlying proposition that our behaviour is significantly determined by beliefs that judge behaviour against a set of universal core values.

The two central and related themes of Systems Leadership are theories of Capability and Culture. We articulate how individuals differ in terms of their ability to cope with complexity of work (capability) but also our common need to form coherent social groups if we are to survive and prosper. It proposes that it is critical to clarify what work is needed to achieve a specific purpose, especially the complexity of that work and consequently how people can make their best contributions. Secondly, we propose underlying principles concerning organisational arrangements that are more likely or less likely to sustain social cohesion and the achievement of that purpose.

If implemented holistically, with discipline and commitment SLT can provide the conditions where people willingly give of their best.

One of our general observations is that people underestimate the impact of organisational arrangements on behaviour. While we are quite used to being precise about technical matters, for example in engineering, medicine, architecture etc, and also precise about commercial matters such as how much people get paid or the costs of materials, we don't seem to think that such precision is relevant to the social arrangements. We use language imprecisely and with different meanings and definitions without recognising how significant that is. Often terms such as culture, leadership, teamwork and even work itself are used differently and often quite vaguely throughout organisations. Systems Leadership offers a precise set of definitions tools and concepts that can be used to analyse and understand why certain organisational arrangements result in creative and productive behaviour while others have the opposite effect.

Just how complex certain work is can be misunderstood. However, by applying the models and concepts we can gain a more detailed understanding of what the work is and whose work it is.

In Systems Leadership we also distinguish between qualitatively different types of social organisation such as meritocracy, democracy, theocrcy and gerontocracy. We look at the significance of these different types of social organisations and how they impact on the way work gets done (or doesn't).

The following accounts are case studies of real organisations coming to grips with the challenges that came, (and remain) with the Covid-19 pandemic. We hope that you find them interesting and helpful when thinking about how to meet such challenges now and in the future.

Different Social and Organisational Responses to the Pandemic

WRITTEN BY IAN MACDONALD

Context and Purpose

In this chapter SLT concepts will be used to analyse responses to the Covid 19 pandemic, especially in the UK and why some have been apparently more or less successful. It is not an exhaustive analysis and recognises that more research would be needed to fully test the hypotheses and propositions. However, the purpose of the paper is to show how SLT concepts can be used to better understand outcomes in order to consider what might be done to improve the situation. It is intended to raise some questions for further discussion. In this paper various SLT concepts will be referred to. It is not within the scope of the paper to explain all of them fully in this text but readers are invited to follow up on a more detailed description in the publication mentioned at the beginning.

Political Leadership and Governmental Response

Clearly the pandemic has had a massive and disruptive impact across the world. The leadership of all sorts of organisations, governmental, public service, small and large businesses and international organisations have tried to address the issues arising from the spread of this virus. What is clear is that some organisations seem to have been much more successful in addressing these critical issues.

There appears to be a very wide variation in outcomes in different countries. For the purpose of this discussion I am only going to discuss a few of those outcomes and measures. The first is deaths per million in different countries. Most people will be aware that simple comparisons are difficult and potentially misleading. There are different methods of data collection, reporting, testing and recording. Countries differ significantly not only in their geographical position, and hence the season of year that the virus has struck but also differences of demographics, poverty, ethnicity and time of onset. However, despite these variables there do appear to be wide disparities between countries that do not seem to be so different in terms of those variables.

If we look at so-called "liberal democracies", where there are less likely to be deliberate attempts to suppress or change the data or significant restrictions in its reporting, we still see wide variation. As of August 6th 2020 deaths per million put Belgium at the top with 863, followed by the UK in second place with 695, Spain in fourth with 609, Italy fifth with 582, Sweden sixth with 565, USA at eighth with 483, France in tenth place with 450 and Ireland in thirteenth with 362. Moving much further down the list we see Germany with 110, Denmark with 106, Finland with 60 and much further down Australia with 10 and New Zealand with 4.5 (These figures are of course changing daily and so are presented as indicative rather than a final table of results).

If we look at total deaths on the same date we find the UK in fourth place, much higher than many other countries with a much larger populations. Why might this be?

Capability of Leaders

One possibility that has been proposed is that countries with women leaders fare much better then countries with male leadership. In a recent study (July 2020), published by the Centre for a Economic Policy Research and the World Economic Forum, evidence was produced to demonstrate this. A study from John Hopkins University compared countries with women leaders with similar countries with male leaders: New Zealand with Ireland, Germany with the UK and Bangladesh with Pakistan. The data, particularly on deaths per hundred thousand was starkly in favour of the countries led by women.

While this data points to the relative success of Germany with Angela Merkel, New Zealand with Jacinda Ardern, Denmark with Mette Frederiksen, Taiwan's Tsai Ing-wen and Finland with Sanna Marin, it would be very unlikely, without wanting to detract from their achievements, that a single variable will explain the variation. In a very informative article published in The Atlantic by Helen Lewis (May 6, 2020), while acknowledging that such women have done a good job, she points to the relative failure of the so-called "strong, macho leadership style" demonstrated for example in the USA, Brazil and the UK. Here simplistic assertions, denials and blaming others has been exposed as not only ineffective but deadly. Lewis also points out that the positive qualities and behaviours demonstrated by such women leaders are also evident in male leaders. She cites Justin Trudeau as an example, but others too have demonstrated empathy and an ability to create collaborative, productive teams. The analysis of 194 countries (Centre for Economic Policy Research ibid) reported that in the countries led by women such results indicated "the proactive and co-ordinated policy responses adopted by female leaders."Also, "our results clearly indicate that women leaders reacted more quickly and decisively in the face of potential fatalities".

In SLT we identify five elements of capability: Mental Processing Ability: (MPA), Knowledge, Technical Skills, Social Process Skills:(SPS) and Application combining to result in work outcomes. My hypothesis would be that, even in liberal democracies women have had a much tougher time reaching high-level positions whether elected or appointed. As a result of this it is more likely that women in such leadership roles actually have a higher MPA, and therefore ability to deal with complexity than many of their male counterparts. This will also indicate higher capability with regard to system design and in particular the integration of systems to create coherence. Also it is probable that such women have had to develop social process skills across broader groups than their male counterparts. It may also be that such women are more likely to identify with the purpose of leadership: to change behaviour to achieve an outcome, rather than simply having the purpose of *being in power.*

Entitlement and Meritocracy

In the UK the current Prime Minister is one of a succession of Eton, Oxbridge, educated males, who along with colleagues past and present (such as David Cameron, George Osborne, Jacob Rees-Mogg and others), very understandably and rationally assume they are entitled by birth and background to occupy such positions of power.

In the UK 7% of children are educated at private schools. Of Britain's 55 Prime Ministers 20 were educated at Eton, a further 7 came from Harrow and 6 from Westminster. There has been a grand total of 9 that have been educated at one of the other 4,188 state secondary schools. Currently two thirds of the Cabinet were privately educated. By contrast Ardern, Merkel, Frederiksen and Marin were all educated at state schools.

Good social process skills are less needed if you have powerful networks and precedent. Application is needed but again perhaps not as much when you have the inside track. Assertiveness and supreme confidence can mislead some to believing this is evidence of high MPA. Similarly, a good education and consequential acquisition of knowledge can give the appearance of high MPA. Certainly in the UK a private education that includes classics can also superficially look like high MPA.

Such qualities can appear impressive until real, highly complex work is required. It is then that the "right words" and soundbites are exposed as superficial.

Systems and System Design

Systems Leadership self evidently stresses the importance of the design and integration of systems as essential leadership work. This is complex work. Our definition of work; turning intention into reality, also mirrors the relationship between policy and systems. Policies are a statement of intent, systems turn that intent into reality. It is not sufficient for a leader to annunciate policy but then not understand how or if the resulting systems will deliver the purpose of the policy.

A recent example of this has been the new system that has been designed to calculate and allocate grades for A-level exams in the UK. Despite knowing for around five months that students would not be able to sit exams and consequently an alternative system would be needed to assess performance. It was not until after the system, commissioned by the government and designed by Ofqal (a government education regulator) had produced its results that the Minister for Education responded to the almost universal criticism of its unfairness. He claimed that it was not his fault as he was not aware of how the system would actually work. The sudden shift to teacher assessments then occurred after the event with consequential chaos as grades were overturned and university entrance was severely disrupted. It is the schools and universities that are now left to sort out the mess whilst Ofqal has been scapegoated.

Thus, in order properly to address the many and complex problems associated with a pandemic there is a desperate need for well-designed and integrated systems that have to be designed and implemented in a unique situation. This is especially the case as previous governments have not properly prepared for such a significant Critical Issue as this pandemic. (A Critical Issue is one, which if not anticipated and planned for, will cause an existential threat). When system design has to be done live, rather than in anticipation of a problem, the complexity, and consequence increases.

In the UK the availability, or lack of availability of PPE is but one example of a lack of foresight, despite warnings, and helps explain why the problem became more complex than it needed to be. As we know from SLT designing effective systems, especially on a national scale, that not only work in their own right but are integrated with other systems and on a national scale requires the mental processing ability starting at complexity IV and then of at least V and VI to be successful. There is little evidence that such MPA exists in the ministerial work of the UK government nor that the complexity of the problem has been properly recognised.

As a consequence, systems have been introduced on a piecemeal basis, one at a time and with little or no integration with other systems. Currently there are at least two test and trace systems, one a Public Health England system, with approximately an 83% success rate in tracking contacts, while the new privately contracted National track and trace system, run by the private company Serco at a cost of around £10 billion, has at best around a 50% success rate of even contacting people (no figures exist about whether they then self-isolate). The information gained from this second system is not available to the first and the centralised database until recently could not be accessed locally.

At the time of writing it has just been announced that the Public Health England organisation has been disbanded and replaced by another (National Institute for Health Protection) to be headed by the person in charge of the (flawed) national test and trace system. Jeremy Farrar, the director of the Welcome Trust commented; "ill thought through, short term reactive reforms....Response to singular crisis without strategic vision".

Other examples include the on/off system of quarantining incoming international passengers, the wearing or not wearing of facemasks, the numbers of people you can or cannot meet, the rule that you could have a cleaner in your house but not a member of your family. This does not suggest high-level MPA applied to system design. Thus, the complexity of system design has been underestimated in the UK and I would suggest this would be a common problem in any country that has a relatively high death rate.

Advisory Relationships

Most governments have at least consulted relevant scientists, including those who have studied pandemics and contagious diseases. However, the relationship between the two is not always clear. In any governmental process, scientists should only ever be advisors, however the popular phrase 'following the science' can be ambiguous. It can mean both listening to the scientific advice and making judgements accordingly or at the same time automatically making decisions on the basis of this advice. In this way politicians can claim success when it goes well but blame scientists if it goes badly. We have seen this before in the case of the invasion of Iraq (2003) where the justification was made on the basis of apparent intelligence information (later discredited).

If we are to understand the nature and authority in such organisations then politicians should be held accountable for their own judgement and decisions. An advisory relationship is just that; providing advice not making decisions.

Oversimplification

When we examine the political process; it is often characterised by slogans, symbols and rhetoric that oversimplify the problem. "Get Brexit Done" was hugely successful without clarifying what that meant in detail or seriously estimating what cost it might incur. Another approach used widely by the current government in the UK, (but not exclusively) is the continued use of metaphor alone. Populist leaders appear to be satisfied simply with the metaphor or slogan and leave the detail to someone else, who can be blamed later if it goes wrong.

One example was one of the original UK government three words slogans "Protect the NHS". When we look at purpose statements they should be able to give clarity as to what behaviour should achieve that purpose. This simple slogan then led to many patients being discharged from NHS hospitals into care homes to make the beds available for potential Covid patients. Patients were discharged without being tested into care homes with disastrous results. It also seemed a strange slogan as surely the NHS is meant to protect us. The consequence of poor alignment between Systems Symbols and Behaviours, (a core part of the culture model in SLT) has had deadly consequences.

Systems, Symbols and Behaviour

SLT puts these forward as the three tools of leadership which should be used together if leadership is to be effective. We have often seen them used individually or missing out one. From examples above this either does not work or is not sustainable.

On 28 April 2020 the Guardian newspaper in the UK published an article that I wrote concerning the NHS. The definition of work in SLT is as mentioned, "turning intention into reality". It is based upon Elliott Jacque's definition of work where he emphasises the use of discretion, human judgement and decision making in creating the pathway or methodology that will achieve a specified output. In the article I argued that the use of symbolic language like saints, miracle workers, and heroes allows us to avoid thinking about the necessary complex work done by people in the professions and instead imagine them being successful because of their religious vocation or magic superpowers. I also argued that the ritualistic weekly applause for the NHS staff (and then eventually other key workers) while well-intended was actually to make us feel better. The article pointed out the hypocrisy of politicians joining in this public ritual even though for years they had voted against public sector improvement in conditions. They actually governed over a period of time where these so-called miracle workers actually experienced an effective reduction in pay. This article stimulated a lot of response and agreement that symbolic responses without an underlying system or behaviour change is clearly cosmetic.

Accountability

However, does any of this matter? The use of political spin and distraction may be designed to give the appearance of doing something while substance is lacking. Accountability in the political process is far different from that in an executive hierarchy or meritocratic organisation. The simplification of complex problems and the illusion that they have been solved are tricks well-known and well-practised by many politicians. A related approach has been to shift discussion onto targets rather than discuss purpose or why those targets matter. In the early months of the pandemic there were constant promises with regard to the number of daily tests. There was quite misleading data (which was admonished by the Office of National Statistics) in this area as government numbers variously referred to capacity, not actual tests (capacity is still being quoted at the time of writing), tests sent out rather than necessarily tests completed, repeat testing of the same people. Whatever the merits or otherwise this distracted from the purpose of testing. The relative failure of various contact tracing systems announced with such fanfare as a "world beating" still remain poorly but expensively implemented. As one member of the public interviewed on the BBC News said recently; "we don't need it to be world-beating, we just need it to work!"

Next another system designed to provide face-masks for NHS staff revealed that 15 million masks were actually unsuitable for use. The Guardian reported that the order was part of a £252 million supply contract awarded to an investment firm in April. This investment firm, Ayanda Capital, describes itself as specialising in currency trading, offshore property, private equity and trade financing. Other contracts identified by the Good Law Project identified similar contracts with variously; a pest control company, a confectioner and a family hedge fund. Contracts are able to be awarded without tender or scrutiny under the emergency rules operating during a pandemic. There is however precedent for this type of behaviour as it is reminiscent of a notorious case where during the Brexit negotiations the government transport minister, Chris Grayling, awarded a multi-million pound ferry contract to a company that had no ferries! These emergency powers serve to avoid accountability, certainly in real time.

Accountability for political processes are of course primarily through elections, every five years, but also monitored by a free press and the judiciary. It is also interesting to note that the strongman macho model of politics, referred to by Helen Lewis in the Atlantic article, is also typified by attacks on precisely these institutions; the press ("fake news") and the judiciary (referred to as "the enemy of the people" in a Daily Mail headline when they declared the prorogation of Parliament illegal in December 2019). Already the current UK government has announced a major judicial review and a review of the funding of the BBC.

In June 2020 Sir Mark Sedwell agreed to step down as Cabinet Secretary. At that time an article in the Independent newspaper (online) was published: "Sir Mark's departure comes amid plans for a wide ranging shakeup of Whitehall driven by the ambitions of Mr Johnson's top aide Dominic Cummings to streamline the civil service machine. It is certain to be seen as a bid by Johnson and Cummings to get their own people into key positions at the heart of the Downing Street operation.....

Liberal Democrat acting leader Ed Davey said the prime minister appeared to be indulging his adviser's wish to politicise the civil service."

Dave Penman, head of the FDA union for top civil servants commented: "no CEO or chair of a private company would act in this way and expect their organisation to thrive. A government that so publicly covets the best of the private sector on delivery could do with learning exactly what good leadership looks like: it certainly isn't this."

Mythologies

SLT uses the term mythology to describe what many people might refer to as beliefs or attitudes. We have used that term because it refers to the rationale we use to interpret behaviour as being positive or negative on the universal values continua. It is intended to reflect the reality that our judgements are a combination of logic and emotion. The Universal Values Continua is our typology of six universal human experiences that rate or judge all behaviours systems and symbols heuristically. Whenever we see elections we will see these universal values referred to. Who do we trust? Who tells us the truth? Who has the courage to make difficult decisions? Do our lives matter (love/respect)? Will legislation be fair? The popularity or otherwise of political parties is determined by our judgements against these universal values.

During the pandemic governments worldwide have demonstrated their authority and an ability to control human behaviour. New laws and regulations have required significant changes to behaviour almost instantly. Such rules are highly specific about when or where we can go out, go to work, meet others, congregate, shop and many other aspects of daily life. Such requirements cannot be universally enforced or monitored solely by the police and/or by the army. Compliance is largely dependent upon clarity of those rules and an acceptance that, although difficult, they are for mutual benefit; they rate positively on the values continua. Finally, acceptance is dependent upon them being systems of equalisation that is they apply to all people in the same way. If these criteria are met there is evidence, from the recent pandemic that there is significant compliance without recourse to legal action.

Although in the UK there has been criticism with regard to a lack of clarity, by and large there has been significant compliance. That is, until the Prime Minister's closest advisor, Dominic Cummings, made his notorious, 264 mile trip to Durham during lockdown and when infected with Covid 19. Research at University College London: Covid 19 Social Study revealed that willingness to adhere to lockdown guidelines dropped after this incident and more steeply in England than in

Scotland and Wales. It was not simply the fact of breaking lockdown rules; The Lancet piece notes; "although some other officials and senior figures had also broken the lockdown rules, this transgression was the first to occur with no apology and no resignation". Dr Daisy Fancourt was quoted as saying, " it is the biggest step change without a rebound across the whole period". A YouGov survey found that of those who had broken lockdown rules, one in three gave the Cummings story as a justification and the phrase "doing a Cummings" has become part of the language of the pandemic in the UK.

National Mythologies

Although a global phenomenon the pandemic has been dealt with on a national basis. The term lockdown has become familiar in most countries although it has varied in detail.

How we perceive this pandemic and how we address it has also varied by country. In SLT, as mentioned above, we point to the significance of mythologies in determining our behaviour. While no two individuals share an exact set of mythologies we do form cultures on the basis of significant overlap with regard to those mythologies. Cultures form in families, organisations, religions and in every socially cohesive group. When reviewing the approach taken in the UK it is perhaps worth noting what we might call National Mythologies. That is a set of stories and beliefs that we tell ourselves and each other to reinforce positive culture that will maintain social cohesion and binds us together, especially in the face of adversity. Some might say these are simply national stereotypes, but in SLT we are interested in a more detailed approach and linking that to specific systems, symbols and behaviour.

As with any social group, mythologies will not remain constant. Although they do not disappear they are superseded by new, more functional mythologies. In the UK the Brexit debate certainly exposed quite a wide range of mythologies about our cultural identity in the UK and our trust or otherwise of "foreigners" and outsiders. So, what can we use? Britain and in particular England has been calling upon mythologies used in the Brexit debate. The essence of this belief recalls (or conjures up) a courageous country standing alone in the Second World War against a far greater enemy. Because of our character, stoicism and loyalty we can apparently overcome anything. Despite a great deal of evidence that England and the UK have rarely if ever fought any war or been successful in any conflict without significant alliances, including the Second World War, (perhaps excluding the Falklands War) the strength of this mythology is remarkable. The use of Winston Churchill as a symbol demonstrating this lone defiance has continued through Brexit to this pandemic despite the fact that Churchill, like many world leaders in war, was desperate to form alliances and actually called for the establishment of a political European alliance after the war precisely to prevent further conflict.

What this mythology has served to do is to create an illusion that beating this virus is about individual courage and character, that we don't need bureaucratic systems or detailed analysis. Individual effort will win the day. This was also demonstrated by the Prime Minister boasting that despite warnings, he had shaken hands with people suspected of being positive in hospital. A couple of weeks later he was in intensive care.

The popularity of this Second World War mythology has been most obviously demonstrated by the example of "Captain Tom", the Second World War veteran who on 6 April 2020 set out to walk around his garden at the age of 99 with his walking frame hoping to raise £1000 for NHS charities before his hundredth birthday. His embodiment of the national mythology was clearly evident in that he raised £32.79 million! He was promoted to honorary Colonel and on 17th July knighted personally by the Queen for his efforts. I do not wish to decry this extraordinary, and heartwarming, personal achievement but merely to show this as an example of the power of national mythologies. Unfortunately, such mythologies are not necessarily all that is needed to defeat a virus.

More systematic approaches like those taken in Germany have re-sulted in relative success. Not surprisingly the Germans have made great efforts to create new national mythologies after the Second World War. These stories (understandably) do not invoke the imagery of war and conflict but are about efficiency, hard work and negotiation. Finland, Australia and New Zealand also have not drawn so heavily on such ad-versarial symbols during this pandemic. As Helen Lewis says they take a more inclusive approach.

Meritocracies

This critique does not suggest that there are no organisations in the UK that are addressing issues or designing systems at level IV complex-ity and above. What is being proposed is that they are doing this despite the centralised government approach rather than because of it. Since the pandemic, schools have had over 250 different changes in instruc-tions as to how they should organise to remain open, social distance and bring in staff and pupils. However, headteachers and their leadership teams throughout the country have worked out for themselves how to design relatively safe systems while under considerable stress. They have designed systems that have had to take into account the safety of chil-dren, the safety of staff, the families and local community.

The NHS leadership and management, care home organisers and lo-cal authorities have had to design their own systems because of the in-adequacy of the national systems. These organisations are meritocracies and as such have recognised that planning for service delivery in a chang-ing context is complex work. By and large people in those roles have demonstrated their capability. However they are rarely consulted before new constraints are announced. There has been a tendency to ignore or underestimate local knowledge and capability. At the time of writing the local authority of Preston in the north of England, like Blackburn and Darwin has had to design its own testing and tracing system because of the inadequacies of the national system when a new lockdown has been imposed by the government. Such system design is not Box C (see systems matrix) because they are not unauthorised. The national "systems" do not really work effectively as such. They tend to be constraints or rules often with very little help as to how they might be implemented. Of course we might expect that the Civil Service should be doing the system design, and that it is designed to be a meritocracy. However government announcements have often taken them by surprise too. It is difficult for the Civil Service to work effectively if the government is simply reacting to events. "Making it up as you go along" seems to be the order of the day, or as we might say leadership at level II or at best III with little evidence of IV +.

As we have mentioned work is turning intention into reality. It is largely organisations that are designed on the principle that people are appointed to roles on the basis of capability rather than nepotism, seniority or election that has carried the load in fighting this pandemic. In the UK such organisations have different structures, systems and are more used to strategic and detailed planning, and hence turning intention into reality.

One multi-national organisation; AngloAmerican uses SLT as the basis for its organisational model and SLT underpins the way it is structured and led. (For details of their business and countries where they operate see their website)

The CEO, Mark Cutifani, occupies a Level VII role and his direct reports are expected to work at Level VI. The businesses are largely run at Level V and the model of complexity (Levels of Work) informs the work of the role. When it became clear that the pandemic was indeed worldwide and would affect the entire business and all employees a task was assigned to design systems that would mitigate those effects. The work was assigned to members of the Sustainability Committee (already existing) and two members (in Level VI roles) consulted and designed an integrated, world wide set of systems. They categorised the work in four areas: Physical Health, Mental Health, Living with Dignity (covering for example partner violence and shelter/accommodation) and

Community Response Plans. It is not possible in this paper to go into an indepth account of the approach, however it is reasonable to say that the approach included very clear communication and an integrated set of systems for all parts the organisation worldwide.

They have ensured sufficient and available supplies of PPE, available regular testing and tracing, support not only for employees but families and communities and continued to run the business albeit with limitations.

Clearly such an organisation does not have the range of responsibilities as a government, including for example education and defence. Without suggesting AngloAmerican is perfect it does demonstrate that a coherent and effective response can be managed across borders and between organisations inside and outside the company. One of the most striking qualities of the AngloAmerican "Covid-19 WeCare" response was the creation of a reporting system that actually reported on what had actually been achieved and was being achieved; rather than overly optimistic pronouncements about what is going to happen with little evidence as to how that is going to be achieved.

Summary

This paper has explored the way that this pandemic has been addressed through the lens of Systems Leadership. Addressing this pandemic requires work not simply denial, exhortation, promises or slogans.

It is clear that political decisions over the last 5-10 years have discounted the identification of a pandemic as a critical issue and therefore the need for stockpiling PPE and having drafted, emergency policies and systems to call on.

Perhaps most significantly the complexity of the work required to address this pandemic has been under estimated. Specifically, the complexity of designing national systems and systems that are integrated rather than ad hoc and fragmented.

If the 20 questions of system design (ref: p247 Systems Leadership ibid) had been applied to such systems they may have been designed and implemented in a much more effective way and resulted in less deaths. The Prime Minister's so-called "whack-a-mole" strategy perhaps actually and symbolically typifies this undisciplined approach.

While national mythologies are functional in creating social cohesion they may be less so in dealing with problems that cannot be overcome simply by willpower and character.

We can also see that organisations that are set up to do work and organised on the basis of meritocracy are better able to deal with such problems although never perfect. Of course, this is why we have an intended meritocratic civil service to enact government policy but we can also see that where this civil service has been politicised or overridden by unelected government advisors it is less successful in doing real work.

SLT exposes the potential conflict between a meritocratic executive and political appointees. This is of course not exclusive to the UK. However it raises the question of purpose. In SLT we compare a royal court with a meritocracy. In the court, like any political process the work of staying in power can dilute or conflict with the achievement of externally verifiable outputs. Real work can be pushed aside. Unfortunately the price of avoidance of real work in this pandemic is unnecessary death, especially for vulnerable groups.

Addendum: August 2021

Since this article was written there have of course been a lot of changes in the rate and spread of the virus and its variants leading to different responses. The cherished major Tom has sadly passed away and Dominic Cummings power came to an end when he was sacked by the British Prime Minister, but not for his infamous Trip. Cummings has since asserted his opinions with regard to the lack of capability of his former boss.

The evidence of an integrated systemic approach is still lacking in the UK. The government has continued to adopt a single system solution; vaccination as their salvation.

Differences in approach worldwide seem to have become more extreme with the entire country of New Zealand being locked down as a result of a single case whereas there are virtually no restrictions in the UK despite a daily death rate of almost 100 and daily cases running at around 30,000 per day.

2

The "Ruby Princess" – the complexity of systems design

WRITTEN BY GEOFF MCGILL

Context

The passenger cruise ship Ruby Princess, operated by Princess Cruises, docked in Sydney in the early hours of 19 March 2020, having cut short a cruise to New Zealand, begun on 8 March. Two thousand seven hundred and sixty passengers disembarked later that morning despite concerns about Covid-19 (CV-19). Thirteen passengers had been tested for CV-19. Not all results were available at disembarkation.

More than 600 Ruby Princess passengers later tested positive to CV-19. At least 35 were international cases. The eventual outcome was 900 cases (700 passengers/191 crew) and 28 people died.

CV-19 subsequently spread in Australia. An Australian example was at Tasmania's North West Regional Hospital with the first cases detected on 3 April. By 21 April, 114 people had contracted CV-19 – 73 hospital staff, 22 patients, and 19 others.[1]

The Key Players

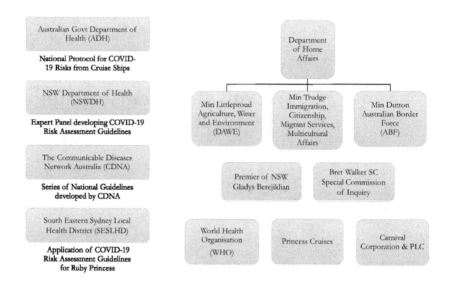

Special Commission of Inquiry

On 15 April 2020, the Special Commission of Inquiry (SCI) into the Ruby Princess was established by the NSW Government, led by Commissioner Bret Walker SC. The terms of reference were to inquire into and report on:

"The knowledge, decisions and actions of Ruby Princess crew, medical staff and the ship operator, Princess Cruises, with respect to cases or potential cases of respiratory infections on the ship.

The information provided to, communications between, and decisions and actions of Commonwealth and NSW agencies, including the Australian Border Force, the Federal Department of Agriculture, Water and the Environment, NSW Health, the NSW Police Force, NSW Ambulance and the Port Authority of NSW.

Policies and protocols applied by Princess Cruises and Commonwealth and NSW Government agencies with respect to managing suspected or potential COVID-19 cases.

Communications by Commonwealth and NSW Government agencies to passengers disembarking the Ruby Princess.

Full terms of reference are **Attachment 1.** The SCI transcript and exhibits can be accessed at *www.rubyprincessinquiry.nsw.gov.au*

Federal Court Action

Passengers initiated legal action against Carnival Plc and Princess Cruise Lines Ltd over the handling of CV-19 cases on the Ruby Princess. It is alleged the companies breached consumer guarantees, engaged in misleading and deceptive conduct and failed in their duty of care to provide a safe cruise. [2]

A duty of care is also owed to crew members, but they are not represented in this action. The SCI terms of reference did not cover the standard of care given to the welfare and interests of crew members. The SCI specifically noted this omission.[3]

The NSW Police also initiated an investigation as to whether criminal negligence was involved; this was on-going on 14 August 2020 when the SCI Report was released.

Economic Importance

Cruise ships are one of the fastest growing sectors of the Australian Tourism Industry, an industry estimated to be $5.2 billion in 2018/2019 alone. In 2016/2017, NSW accounted for nearly 60%. This added pressure to the context in which events unfolded. Delays in the turnaround of passenger cruise ships and special accommodation arrangements to manage quarantine needs come at considerable costs to the private entities, government agencies and ultimately taxpayers.[4]

Insights from the Special Inquiry

From the SCI, it is evident that the authority, accountability and roles in granting pratique ,that is, the clearance given to an incoming ship by the health authority of a port, were far from clear. As a result the application of the risk assessment procedures for controlling infectious disease on cruise ships failed spectacularly.[5]

Yet, before this tragic event, in the context of the emerging pandemic, a new protocol was developed in early 2020, specifically to respond to the public health risks associated with CV-19. The public health experts thought they knew the risks associated with the management of this disease. The new protocol was based on the risk assessment system using clinical and epidemiological criteria for other known infectious diseases such as influenza. These procedures were not strictly applied in practice. Furthermore, the SCI found applying past practice in the context of the Covid-19 virus was a seriously flawed approach.

Purpose of the Case Study

This case study examines human decision making in the context of a sharp spike in complexity in the operating environment of managing cruise ship entry into Australian Ports, during a pandemic. It is about how flaws in system design, lack of clarity on how different systems interface and integrate, lead to system failure. It intends to show how ambiguity in the required work and the discretion to be exercised, can lead to disastrous outcomes even with the best intentions. The case study draws on Systems Leadership Theory (SLT) principles and models to illuminate how this can happen and how it can be avoided.

The SCI's final report of 14 August 2020 indicated that some decisions, especially those made by the NSW Health Department (NSWDH), were as inexplicable as they were inexcusable. The Premier of NSW, Gladys Berejiklian, in her initial response to the report noted it was fortunate Mr Walker had not identified any systemic issues within the state's health authorities.[6]

The SLT analysis advanced in this study cannot support this position. Using the lens of SLT, the outcomes become explicable and predictable.

Scope and Timeline

This case study reviews evidence before the SCI into the Ruby Princess, the key conclusions, recommendations and the scope and method of inquiry of the SCI itself. It critiques actions, decisions and errors of omission made by the key players involved. An assessment of what is required at the national level is also provided.

The earlier voyages of Princess Cruise Line ships with CV-19 cases form important context. On 20 January, the Diamond Princess left Yokohama on a 16-day voyage. CV-19 was identified in Hong Kong on 1 February, the vessel subsequently quarantined off Okinawa. By 20 February, cases had surged to 634. Repatriation of passengers began; on 20 February 164 Australian passengers arrived at the Howard Springs facility in the Northern Territory. Concerns about CV-19 increased in February and March with the voyage of the Grand Princess from California. Test samples from 45 passengers were taken by helicopter to the Centre for Disease Control in the US. When advised of a positive case, the Grand Princess cancelled all social activities planned for the journey.[7]

These events prompted Carnival Plc to set up a monitoring group headed by an Incident Commander to respond to further potential CV-19 threats. When the Ruby Princess left Sydney on 8 March, Carnival Plc knew the risk management issues.

Public Health professionals in Australia were also closely studying the clinical and epidemiological characteristics of the virus. During the first months of 2020, several iterations of guidelines and protocols for managing the risks associated with CV-19 had been developed.

The events leading up to the voyage of the Ruby Princess on 8 March and the 8-19 March voyage itself are sufficient for understanding, through the lens of SLT, what the SCI described as inexplicable is explicable.

Timeline of Key Events February - March 2020

17 March Ruby Princess's Doctor also unaware of updated **CDNA guidelines**. Some instances of influenza like illness prompt **first** announcement for passengers feeling unwell to come for medical assessment.

On the basis of a spike in cases picked up on **17 March** through Carnival's central monitoring systems, it had anticipated Ruby Princess would be assessed medium to high risk.

February – March
NSWDH Expert Panel developing COVID-19 Risk Assessment Guidelines following CDNA guidelines.

8 March Ruby Princess departs after health screening 59 passengers.

19 March Ruby Princess docks in Sydney, pratique granted and all passengers disembark with some boarding interstate and international flights.

Jan, Feb – March Earlier voyages of Diamond Princess and Grand Princess.

Series of National Guidelines developed by CDNA.

By **10 March** , the criteria for a "suspect case" of COVID-19 had been updated to include all international travel in the 14 days before the onset of illness. Definition had been in place for in **excess of one week prior to the risk assessment expert panel formed by NSW Health for Ruby Princess.**

11 March WHO made the assessment that COVID-19 is a pandemic.

18 March. Application of COVID-19 Risk Assessment Guidelines for Ruby Princess South Eastern Sydney Local Health District (SESLHD). Assessed as low risk but ARD log from Ruby Princess not up to date and CDNA epidemiological Guidelines not updated. MoU between DAWE and NSWDH not followed, Traveller with Illness Checklist (TIC) procedures not followed.

14 April Special Commission of Inquiry established and reported **15 August.**

Premier concluded on basis of Report there were no systemic issues and NSWDH staff remain in place.

Activities continue as normal with no social distancing including final night celebrations and staff party on board after **pratique** *granted about 6.30am* **19 March.**

Application of Systems Leadership Theory (SLT)

Systems Leadership is a coherent, integrated theory of organisational behaviour. It has a clear leadership model directly related to capability and work complexity of work organisation, structure and systems. Work complexity, particularly related to systems design, illustrates the difficulty of redesigning the system to adequately respond to CV-19 and the task of implementing subsequent changes across multiple jurisdictions. It will show how stakeholders underestimated such complexity.

SLT is used to analyse the decision to grant pratique for the Ruby Princess and examines the organisational culture issues that emerge.

The distinction between Policies and Systems

In SLT, policy or protocol refers to a "statement that expresses the standards of practice and behaviour" required to achieve the intent of the stated policy. A policy statement by itself may encourage people to make the desired changes in behaviour, but sustained change requires systems to implement the policy.

The term system is defined as a "specific framework for organising activities to achieve a purpose. The framework orders the flow of work, data, information, money, people, materials and equipment required to achieve the system's purpose". Systems drive behaviour.[8]

Policies and systems driving the decision to disembark

The design, implementation and operation of the policies and systems to manage the risk to public health arising from CV-19 on cruise ships involved work across multiple Commonwealth and State departments and agencies. It also involved engagement with corporations such as Carnival Plc, the multinational parent of Princess Cruises. While it was recognised an integrated national approach was required from the outset, it was not clear which government agency had the authority necessary to implement the intent of the policy framework developed.[9]

Australian Department of Health National Protocol for managing CV-19 risks from Cruise Ships

On 6 March, the Australian Government Department of Health published a "National Protocol for Managing Novel Coronavirus Disease Risk from Cruise Ships". The Department of Agriculture, Water and Environment (DAWE), the Department of Home Affairs, the Chief Human Biosecurity Officers and the Cruise Lines International Association were consulted. The stated policy purpose is:

"to clarify the intent, responsibility, and required action in responding to coronavirus disease 2019 (COVID-19) risk from cruise ships. It is primarily a border operations protocol. Cruise ships may carry domestic or international travellers who pose human biosecurity risks. This may also lead to the spread of diseases to other travellers, particularly given the population density, the duration of cruises and the mixing patterns of people on board...... This protocol is limited to COVID-19 and has specific measures for assessing the risk of COVID-19 on the ship, screening of passengers and crew if required, and initial management of suspected cases..."

Implementation requires enhanced surveillance and control measures to:

- *"Protect the health of travellers on vessels;*
- *minimise the likelihood of large numbers of infected people returning to Australia and further spreading diseases among the community.*
- *manage the impact on the Australian health system; and*
- *prevent the spread of diseases among populations in cruise voyage destinations."*.[10]

It is primarily a border operations protocol with specific actions for managing CV-19 intended to occur within a broader border protection framework. Implementation depended on many departments, agencies and the cruise ship operators. Multiple systems are involved, each with its specific purpose and expected outcomes. The actions taken needed correct sequencing and strict application by all involved.

Adding to the complexity is the international environment in which cruise ships operate and the novel character of CV-19 that behaves very differently to influenza and with no vaccine for some time.

Turning Policy Intent into Reality – the complex work of Systems Design

SLT emphasises the importance of understanding the level of work complexity involved in the design of systems. Levels of work complexity are described in terms of **work in** a system (Complexity I and II), and **working on** the design of systems complexity (Complexity III, IV, V and VI) (See **Attachment 2**). The Level III – VI descriptors are:

> **III** - "Discerning trends to refine existing systems and develop new systems within a single knowledge field."

> **IV** - "Integrating and managing the interactions between a number of systems."

> **V** - "Shaping and managing an organisation within its environment – maintaining the organisations systems and processes so that it is self-sustaining within that environment."

> **VI** - "Shaping the organisation of the future- creating the ethic on a national and international basis that allows entities to function and manages the relationships between entities of a significantly different character[11]

The work complexity in the border protection framework, including the CV-19 risk management systems, range from Complexity III to V. For management in the medium to longer term, arguably VI.

The 20 Questions of Systems Design

These questions guide the design and implementation of systems. Many help explain events and decisions surrounding the Ruby Princess.[12]

Who is the System Owner?

While issued by the Commonwealth Department of Health (CDH), the implementation of the policy depended on others. Multiple entities were operating multiple systems, interacting and impacting each other. These interfaces needed to operate in an integrated way. A minimum IV complexity system needed to be designed and implemented.[13]

This raises the important question of "who is the owner of the system?" that is, who is the person with the authorised discretion to implement or significantly change the system, not merely propose changes. Clarity of system ownership defines who has authority to ensure implementation and who is accountable when something goes wrong. A lack of clarity will inevitably result in blame shifting and finger pointing.

For example, the CDH had significant technical expertise to provide advice and guidance on public health and epidemiology issues. Yet the CDHC described the policy as primarily about border operations.

The ABF, the NSW Department of Health and other government agencies were involved in the decision authorising disembarkation, formally known as the grant of "pratique". Within 48 hours it was clear several passengers had tested positive for CV-19. In the immediate aftermath, confusion and finger pointing were evident from all involved.

Everyone was aware it was essential not to transmit CV-19 into the wider community. The entities involved thought they were clear on their tasks, yet a major blunder in public health administration occurred.

ABF officers worked within specific systems relating to specific aspects of the Customs Act and the Immigration Act, such as checking passports and other customs control tasks. Effective border operations in the context of CV-19 were a key outcome expected but the ABF role did not involve decisions on health matters, and information on illness was misinterpreted by ABF officers. The ABF's tasks were conducted within single field systems III complexity.

Who did have the formal authority to grant pratique? Who was the system owner? The Commonwealth Government submission states:

"... although pratique appears not to have been formally granted before disembarkation, clearly passengers were permitted to disembark in advance of that occurring and no biosecurity officers sought to prevent passengers from disembarking. In that sense, there was a practical granting of pratique to allow passengers to depart before the biosecurity officer could return to shore ... to allow the MARS (Maritime Arrivals Reporting System) to be updated".

"As described above, non-medically trained biosecurity officers considered that they played a formal rather than substantive role in the management of human health risks associated with cruise ships arriving at the Port of Sydney, and in that context, relied entirely on NSW Health to make an assessment of those risks"[14]

The SCI Commissioner observed:

"the most impressive thing left with me after I did my first reading of the Commonwealth material...they could not or did not identify who granted pratique and in accordance with what procedures."

In the SCI final report, Commissioner Walker is more definitive, stating:

"Notwithstanding that Chief Human Biosecurity Officers (CHBOs) and Human Biosecurity Officers (HBOs) have primary responsibility for clinical assessments in relation to human biosecurity, a Biosecurity Officer (a DAWE officer) grants pratique;"[15]

But while there is agreement a DAWE officer grants pratique, there is still confusion about how this was done and by whom. Finger pointing and efforts to deflect accountability inevitably followed. The Senate Inquiry also had conflicting answers from the Secretary of DAWE.[16]

The Commissioner's conclusion and Senate Inquiry evidence does not seem to align with the merely "formal" rather than "substantive" role assigned to DAWE by the Commonwealth, but this does not mean it was the system owner. DAWE was exercising specific authorities relating to cargo, waste, and ballast water, again III complexity systems. While these were important functions, DAWE was just one of the agencies involved in the overall system. It was not the system owner, but its work overlapped with the Commonwealth and NSW Department of Health.

The Commonwealth Department of Health (CDH) has the primary responsibility for matters of human biosecurity but does not have officers or physicians at Australia's borders. It had entered a Memorandum of Understanding (MoU) with DAWE and NSW Health (NSWDH) for frontline human biosecurity services. The NSW policy, Human Biosecurity Officer Guideline (HBO Guideline) issued 3 March 2017 notes that:

a. *Biosecurity Officers are not medically trained and will contact an HBO when instructed to by the **Traveller with Illness Checklist (TIC)**;*
b. *The HBO is to provide advice to the Biosecurity Officer to determine the possibility of a Listed Human Disease (LHD) being present by a combination of clinical indicators, geographic epidemiological criteria and other exposure risks;*
c. *The HBO may grant or withhold pratique*

In this regard, the Guideline notes:

"Pratique should generally be granted once the assessment is complete, unless there is a compelling reason why it is unsafe to let passengers disembark.

Such a reason might be a genuine belief other passengers were exposed to a [LHD] and themselves need to be identified and assessed before a mass of passengers is allowed to disembark."[17]

The SCI Report concludes that the HBO Guidelines were appropriate, but in practice the links with other systems did not operate as intended.[18]

The Ruby Princess docked in the early hours of 19 March 2020, but DAWE in late February had already decided the administration of the TIC would not occur on those occasions where NSW Health was attending the arrival of a vessel and conducting an onboard health assessment for CV-19 risks. This was contrary to DAWE formal work instructions and the MoU. While there is little doubt the officer involved thought he had the authority to do so, through the lens of SLT, DAWE was not the system owner, and therefore, an unauthorised variation to the system had occurred. SLT predicts that, unless there is absolute clarity about the system owner, unauthorised variations and changes to the relevant system will inevitably occur. What the Commissioner observed about the Commonwealth submission:

"The Commonwealth accepts that the Human Health Inspection carried out by DAWE's Biosecurity Officers plays an important role in the verification of information reported by a cruise ship to MARS and assessing any human health risk prior to granting pratique.

*In relation to the assessment of risk to human health, the Commonwealth, in its Voluntary Submission said that "is a policy outcome that the Commonwealth considers to be critically important and which, in hindsight, should have been pursued by the Commonwealth engaging with NSW Health **at a policy level** to ensure that process is reflected this policy outcome..."*

The Commonwealth acknowledged that Biosecurity Officers at the Port of Sydney were not following DAWE policies and that contrary practices had emerged with Ruby Princess.[19]

Crucially, DAWE had not communicated its February decision to NSWDH nor had NSWDH advised DAWE of its enhanced screening procedure, including when it would **not** be conducting a health risk assessment on board i.e., when the risk assessment for the ship was 'low'.

The Special Commissioner concluded:

"NSW Health had created its own procedures, protocols and standard operating procedures concerning the assessment of public health risks posed by cruise ships but these were not obviously or self-consciously concerned with the State's biosecurity arrangement with the Commonwealth or the role its officers (the CHBO and the HBOs) performed in that arrangement. The result was a disturbing disconnectedness between the Commonwealth's and the State's respective biosecurity operations. There was inadequate communication and coordination between each government's parallel operations."[20]

The Commonwealth's intention to engage *at policy level* with NSWDH implies engaging at a higher level in the organisation structure to enable greater attention to the interfaces with other systems and agencies, producing a better integrated system of minimum IV complexity.

However, unless the system owner is clear and that role has the necessary authorities to require system implementation and operational monitoring in real time, SLT predicts ongoing problems in the system's operation.

Critical Issues to be resolved in the design and operation of systems.

In SLT a Critical Issue is something that threatens achieving the purpose of a task and often called a *"showstopper"*. SLT frames these as "What ifs?" and "How tos?".[21] Let's consider the role of the NSWDH.

NSW Health Department systems design work

In February 2020, the Department began developing an enhanced screening procedure to deal with the public health risk posed by cruise ship arrivals in NSW given the emerging CV-19 pandemic. Working group members were experienced public health professionals and epidemiologists. On 19 February, NSW Health issued "Cruise Ship COVID-19 Assessment Procedure" for NSW.

The working group established a standing Expert Panel of mostly professional experts to decide on the appropriate public health response for each ship. The "high, medium, low" risk assessment procedure was an orthodox approach to responding to a public health risk and was entirely appropriate at the time and consistent with the approach adopted by the CDH. So, what had changed and how did things go wrong?

The SCI examined the work of the Expert Panel; members had raised Critical Issues 5-6 days prior to the issue of 19 February procedure. These included the severe consequences for an individual and the community should even one undetected case of CV-19 leave the ship. Dr Gupta, one of the most experienced experts stated:

"Main point of difference is that in my view, in the current situation is that we should wait for test results irrespective of risk category before announcing pratique. The reason is that operationally, people will still present to EDs, GPs etc and that poses a different set of challenges. Better to be clear that no one has coronavirus before leaving."[22]

This concern was raised and supported by at least two other panel members. Panel leader Professor Ferson thought it unnecessary for the onboard health assessment team to assess persons with respiratory symptoms if they did not have "travel history" to countries of concern. Panel member Dr McAnulty replied:

"[i]t is a lot of work, but it's trying to balance the very low risk with the very big problem if we have a case on a ship. Local Transmission is currently mainland China, but it may change in the future".

This is exactly what happened.

The SCI scrutinised why the Expert Panel did not adopt this approach. Professor Ferson was genuinely concerned about the heavy workload being carried by his team of 70 people across NSW DH, variously engaged in contact tracing, health screening, and supporting CV-19 health risk management at Sydney airport. He was also concerned about holding travellers on board while awaiting test results, which could cause undue disruption to onward travel.

The recent experience of the Diamond Princess in Japan was part of the context in which his decision was made. Travellers were kept on board for an extended period because CV- 19 had been found. This caused a "petri dish" like environment on the ship for the further spread of the virus to passengers and crew. The option of compulsory quarantine in onshore hotels was not available at that time in NSW. The failure to resolve the critical issue Dr Gupta and other team members had raised produced a fatal flaw in the design of the system issued by the Expert Panel. They were saying and the Commissioner ultimately agreed, that in all cases test results must be obtained.[23]

From an SLT perspective, some other issues arise about the work of the Expert Panel. First, was the purpose of the system clearly and succinctly articulated and understood and shared by all panel members? It would be reasonable to conclude, that while not succinctly stated, the

Expert Panel Team had a shared purpose, but the teams from DAWE and ABF, working in their single field Complexity III systems, did not.

Second, all panel members were under extreme work pressures in their individual roles in different work locations. Meetings were conducted through phone conferences and all members could not always attend, drafts were not always provided to all members and, as apparent during the SCI, recollection of discussions at meetings was poor.

If the purpose of the system was to minimise the risk of CV-19 being introduced into NSW by cruise ship passengers and crew, then any concerns about the inconvenience to passengers being delayed on-board while test results were obtained was not a relevant consideration. However, Professor Ferson's decision not to adopt panel members suggestions points to some influence of this consideration.

Third, what was it about the team's culture that allowed this decision to stand? The SCI did not comment, it was reluctant to tell professionals 'How to do their job", but it warrants attention by the leaders of the NSWDH.[24]

Nonetheless, Professor Ferson as the team leader of the Expert Panel, could reasonably be held to account for his decision not to adopt system design ideas within his authority. When the Expert Panel conducted the risk assessment for the Ruby Princess, it was using a flawed system, although the weakness of the "orthodox approach" was not conceded before the SCI.

The NSW authorities did however concede one major error. Changes to the countries from which passengers would be deemed to be "suspect cases" was expanded to all international travel in the last 14 days, which meant the USA was now an included country. This change to the Communicable Diseases Network Australia (CDNA) was not reflected in the "Enhanced Procedures". What insights does SLT provide on "how did this happen?"

Who should be the System Custodian/Designer?

The system custodian is usually an expert in the field in which the system operates, who monitors the system's operation and advises the system owner on recommended changes. Often the custodian will have been involved in its design, usually as part of a systems design team.

The custodian monitors real-time data from the controls, indicating whether the system is operating as intended. Controls are part of system design. positioned where hand offs occur, or a key step happens. The custodian is constantly looking for critical issues emerging from control data. Changes in the context of the system can pose a risk to the purpose and outcome of the system. While the owner and the custodian can be the same person, in large busy operations, a separate role and someone with the capability to manage work of IV complexity is required, precisely because the owner and operations team are flat out. [25]

The NSW Government submission to the SCI describes what happened:

> "On 10 March 2020, the Communicable Diseases Network of Australia (CDNA) amended its definition of a "suspect case" of COVID-19 by expanding the epidemiological criteria to extend to "International travel in the 14 days before illness onset" – that is, all international travel satisfied the epidemiological criteria...
>
> While it is therefore accepted that the 19 February Procedure should have been revised as at 10 March...the lack of change was simply a symptom of the extraordinary pressure all relevant NSW Health personnel were under at the time...The experts engaged by the Commission themselves expressed the opinion that it would have been extremely difficult for public health specialists with multiple responsibilities to keep up with changing definitions...
>
> As all members of the expert panel who carried out the risk assessment of the Ruby Princess on 18 March acknowledged, the change to the CDNA definition of a "suspect case" on 10 March should have been recognised in carrying out the 18 March risk assessment... All panellists accepted before

the Commission that the risk assessment of the Ruby Princess should have been, at least, "medium risk".[26]

The SCI found the decision of the Expert Panel to assess the Ruby Princess as low risk and grant pratique inexplicable. The lens of SLT provides further insights.

First, a system custodian role would have significantly reduced the risk of this oversight. Second, the pressure of work in public health administration can be predicted to continue unless there are key changes in system design and clarity about who is the system owner and custodian. Third, the complexity of the work involved must be understood and reflected in organisation structure, design of roles and appropriately resourced; if not, further errors and rework can be predicted. Finally, the concession that the Ruby Princess should have been assessed at least medium risk, begs the question "is the orthodox system appropriate at all in the context of the novel corona virus, CV-19?". Continuing with this system design ignores the critical issues raised by Expert Panel members before 19 February, which also apply to the CDH procedures. As Commissioner Walker observed in the Report:

"...the infectiousness of SARS-CoV-2 was understood to be such as to mandate taking all reasonable steps to prevent its spread from a cruise ship. Even a so-called "low risk" was never worth running."[27]

The low risk category was redundant, and the grant of pratique as a default presumption was contrary to the cautionary principle concerning CV-19.

The Ruby Princess – CV-19 risk management systems

In reviewing responses to CV-19 the descriptor of V Complexity helps.

Complexity V – Shaping and managing an organisation within its environment – maintaining the organisations systems and processes so that it is self-sustaining within that environment.

In this context, Carnival Plc would be the organisation (multinational) and Princess Cruises a business unit within the corporation; the Ruby Princess is one of the ships it operates. Following the analysis developed in this paper, Carnival is the system owner of the policies and systems developed to deal with infectious diseases, including CV-19. These policies and systems were applicable across all its operations, and Princess Cruises were required to implement and apply the systems giving effect to the policy's intent. Consistent with work of V Complexity, "managing the organisation in its environment", Princess Cruises had sought to influence and input into the development of CV-19 policies by government authorities such as CDH. Similar work would be required in other jurisdictions. Its operations across the world, would need to account for regulatory variations arising and manage the relationships with the different agencies involved. Carnival's policies and systems relating to the health and safety of passengers and crew in this international context would need to be a system of at least IV Complexity. Being a multinational business entity, its health safety systems, would be part of a suite of integrated systems at IV, ranging across the commercial, technical, and social (people) dimensions of the organisation. The overarching system managing the interactions between these systems at IV and the external environment is the V Complexity system defined above.

Carnival's Mission Statement currently says:

"Our mission is to take the world on vacation and deliver exceptional experiences through many of the world's best-known cruise brands that cater to a variety of different geographic regions and lifestyles, all at an outstanding value unrivalled on land or at sea."[28]

The Mission Statement provides the customer value proposition Carnival wishes to deliver. But this is only one dimension of what a Complexity V system must achieve. The system's purpose must be aligned with the Mission Statement. It must also guide the integration of technical and commercial systems into an overall system design, the outcomes of which will sustain the business. The use of the term "sustain" conveys the need for Carnival to operate in a way that meets obligations to regulators in the commercial and technical jurisdictions in which it operates.

At the same time, it must meet its health and safety obligations to passengers and crew. Distilling the system's purpose is not an easy task, but if Carnival just focussed on its current Mission Statement, serious problems were bound to emerge in the context of CV-19. When closely examined, Carnival's response to the pandemic undermined the very essence of the passenger experience Carnival valued so highly in several ways.

Response to the Pandemic

Carnival understood the threat facing its global business model. In response to the pandemic, a global task force was formed. It included a response team led by an "Incident Commander" for all cruise ships whose team closely monitored developments, including on the Ruby Princess.[29]

On duty involved tracking the data from Acute Respiratory Disease (ARD) log that the ship doctor on the Ruby Princess was required to maintain and report to NSW Health, at least 24 hours before port arrival.

From a SLT perspective, the system had a clear owner, at an appropriate level monitoring a crucial system control. In most respects, the system had been designed to implement the "Enhanced Procedure" applying in Australia. So, what did the SCI reveal?

Special Inquiry findings on the Ruby Princess

From 23 January 2020, Carnival released "instructional notices" relating to CV-19 for managing the risk of potentially infectious passengers on a ship. This included a Standardised Traveller's Health Declaration (THD). Notices became more detailed over time and were used to screen passengers and crew. From 5 March notices included information for medical staff on clinical management of suspected CV-19 cases.

All passengers boarding the Ruby Princess on 8 March were required to complete the THD, with 59 passengers screened further because they had answered "yes" to any question on the THD. Questions included travel through or from specified countries in the last 14 days. Any person in contact with a suspected or confirmed case of CV-19 or a person under monitoring for CV-19 would also require further screening. Ultimately all 59 passengers were cleared to board but not tested for CV-19.[30]

The Australian jurisdiction had additional requirements:

- The isolation of suspected cases on board
- Regular announcements encouraging passengers and crew experiencing symptoms to attend the medical centre for assessment which should be free (to encourage more passengers to come forward); and
- The procurement of swabs for the onboard testing of passengers and crew.

The 9 March Enhanced Procedure required the ship's staff to ensure that:

".... Passengers with Acute Respiratory Illness (ARI) / Influenza Like Illness (ILI) who may be infectious are appropriately isolated and provided with alcohol hand rub and face mask. If sharing a cabin, please also

provide roommates with alcohol hand rub and face masks and educate on how to protect themselves."[31]

The Ship's Doctor in her evidence indicated:

"...on the Ruby Princess this meant that passengers and crew who were required to isolate were those that met the "ILI criteria". Those passengers and crew who were required to isolate had their temperature checked over a 24 hour period, and if they no longer had fever, they were released from isolation."[32]

The SCI accepted this practice on the Ruby Princess concluding:

"...the isolation of passengers with respiratory symptoms absent fever was a matter appropriately left to the discretion of the ship's doctor, at least until 10 March. After that date, passengers on the ship with even an ARI fell within the definition of a "suspect case" of COVID-19. This meant, under the CDNA Guidelines, they should be tested for the disease"[33]

The Commissioner concluded that Carnival should have ensured the ship's doctor was made aware of the CDNA Guidelines for suspect cases. The SCI was even more critical of the same oversight by the Expert Panel and NSW Health officials. If a SLT approach were adopted, the 'system custodian' would provide this advice.

Until the penultimate day of the voyage, the only notice to seek medical assessment was posted in each cabin, and Carnival did not advise passengers any such assessment would be free:

"If you experience any symptoms of respiratory illness which may include fever or feverishness, chills, cough, or shortness of breath, please contact the medical centre".[34]

The SCI concluded it was debateable whether the requirement to make regular announcements was met. Evidence established it was not until the penultimate day of the cruise that the Cruise Director made an announcement inviting passengers with respiratory symptoms to attend the medical centre. Following that, the Medical Centre was busy dealing with passengers and crew seeking assessment.

One of the most interesting findings from an SLT perspective goes to the work of Incident Commander, a role akin to the System Custodian, though the role seems to have been for a specific purpose and timeframe rather than on-going as SLT recommends.

On 17 March, the Incident Commander sent an internal email stating:

"Ruby Princess On route to Sydney ETA, 0630 19/03
Ship has seen a significant spike in ARI & ILI cases in the past few days
Last 48 hours ILI – 13
Total count ILI – 30 ARI – 70
It is likely that the NSW PH unit will classify the ship as Medium to High risk on arrival and so this may slow the disembark process as secondary medical screening will almost certainly apply. Therefore, onward travel arrangements could be affected....
[a]s a precautionary measure, sourcing Hotel rooms has been completed should onward travel be affected". [35]

On the same day he received an email from another Carnival employee:

"also Ruby numbers going Beserk in the last 48 hours. I took my eyes off the ball yesterday" [36]

This occurred two days before the Ruby Princess was to arrive, with the information provided to NSW Health on 18 March. The Carnival

System had identified the health risk and foreshadowed actions required. If the ARD log had been examined "with more than a fleeting glance" within NSW Health, the "significant spike" in ARI/ILI cases on the ship would have been apparent to government officials with the authority to withhold pratique. For these reasons, the SCI concluded no criticism be made of the Incident Commander for not contacting NSW Health regarding his observations of the rate of ARI/ILI on the ship.[37]

The Commission does conclude the Incident Commander should have advised the Ship's Doctor of the CDNA changes. Isolation of suspect cases on board would have occurred for those within this category. The changed epidemiological criteria were not communicated to or acted on by the Ruby Princess.[38]

Carnival argued that the obligation was on an Australian Government agency to urge the operator to monitor them. Governments involved need to take up this invitation, but Carnival operates internationally and given the on-going risks arising from CV-19 and future pandemics, cruise ship operators have to assume this as a positive obligation. No amount of finger pointing can change the fact the number of suspect cases escalated dramatically.

Carnival's failure to act on its knowledge of the change in the CDNA guidelines and the spike in ARI/ILI had tragic consequences. Passengers and crew were not told, social life on board continued as normal, the final night party went ahead and even the after party for the crew went ahead after passengers disembarked.[39]

It will be recalled, the Incident Commander's normal role was Senior Vice President, "Guest Experience" for P&O. It is grim irony to observe that the vacation experience of passengers on the Ruby Princess will never be forgotten. But without changes in its operating systems, it may not prove to be exceptional.

Major Flaws in Carnival Plc systems from SLT perspective

In SLT, a basic distinction is between systems of transformation and transportation. Carnival is in the business of transportation, a characteristic of which is systems and processes intended to protect the subject of transportation (goods, material, information, or people) from unintended change. A transformation system is one where there are intended changes, for example, making steel, manufacturing a motor vehicle or the education system from kindergarten to university. Whatever the core activity, transfer or transformation, it is critical in the system design for one to minimise the other. Passengers on the Ruby Princess did not get from A to B or back again safely. For some, the transformation was fatal.[40]

The Incident Commander was a system custodian. However, such a role needs to be separate and on-going and not caught up in detailed and pressured operational matters. There were controls in place, real-time data identifying trends, appropriate action recognised and yet not actioned. Given his normal role, the Incident Commander seems to have been inherently conflicted.

Transportation vs Transformation tension must be resolved

In SLT, the purpose of the system should be articulated in a single sentence without an "and". Conflict will inevitably arise if two purposes co-exist, resolution of this is essential to the work of system design. In this study, the Carnival system is at V complexity but no purpose statement guiding the design of a system of that complexity is apparent. The Mission Statement seems an implicit, if not an explicit, purpose of the system. If that was the case, conflicting outcomes were inevitable.

In practice, a transportation system failed to minimise the negative and transformative impact of CV-19 on passengers. A conflict clearly arose between the mission and purpose to deliver an exceptional passenger experience and the need for that to be done safely. If not resolved,

SLT would predict Carnival will not succeed in the longer term. Hopefully, Carnival and others in the industry are turning to this work.

Special Commission of Inquiry into Ruby Princess – a thorough audit of only part of the problem.

One of the 20 questions for systems design *"Is there an effective audit process?"* is not consistently adopted in practice. All systems need external audit from time to time, as part of the system design process initiated by the system owner. Audit is a form of control checking the system is working as intended or whether, in the event of changes in the operating context, the system's original purpose is still relevant. The epidemiological and clinical criteria designed into the Enhanced Procedures by the CDH are good examples of system controls.[41]

For the Ruby Princess, the above question needs addressing but the threshold question remains as to who is the system owner? The NSW Government and its respective agencies are only part players in a national system. The SCI Terms of Reference were limited in this respect, as was evidenced in the decision of the Australian Government to make a voluntary statement to the Inquiry. The Commonwealth refused to allow the employees involved in critical decisions to be examined by the SCI. The Commonwealth's policies and systems for management of CV-19 risks have not been subject to the level of public scrutiny applied to other parties appearing before the SCI.

While the SCI makes important conclusions and recommendations, the immediate government responses continued the finger pointing and shifting of blame. The then Commonwealth Minister for Home Affairs, Mr Dutton, claimed vindication over his department's role, pointing to the SCI's criticisms of New South Wales Health officials.[42]

The response of the NSW Premier that no systemic issues arise for its relevant departments and agencies is, on the basis of this case study, not supportable. However, the NSW Government does not have the authority to fix all of the widespread problems. The key Australian Government policy, the National Protocol for managing CV-19 risks from cruise ships, is described by the Federal Health Department as "primarily a border operations protocol".

Rather than using the limited authority and role of the ABF as an excuse to deflect criticism, the on-going lack of clarity of authority and ownership of the border operations protocol is part of the problem. This provides insight into the complex systems design work that remains outstanding.

Observations on the systems design work to be done

Complexity VI work is:

*"Shaping the organisation of the future- creating the **ethic** on a national and international basis that allows entities to function and manages the relationships between entities of a significantly different character" (emphasis added)*

SLT guiding principles and concepts have been used to offer insights and observations from a perspective different from the SCI.

Carnival Plc

First, a systems design task is essential to the future of Carnival Plc and must be done. Covid-19 is an existential threat to it and the cruise ship industry. The analysis of Carnival's current systems suggests there are already some strong foundations in place, with some characteristics of its systems aligning with SLT principles of systems design. For example, the Incident Commander was able to anticipate and predict the actions required on arrival at Sydney.

Second, as has been observed in other large multinational organisations in recent times, such as Rio Tinto and the Juuken Gorge, decisions and omissions have caused enormous reputational damage, particularly raising questions about their ethical basis. SLT posits ethical judgments are fundamental to the work of leaders at Level VI in organisations at the national and international level; it shapes the reputation of the organisation for years to come. It requires creating new assumptions and beliefs about these companies by the community, stakeholders, and customers. The cultural change required must come from the top and requires changes in systems, symbols, and behaviours.[43]

Third, relationships on a national and international level with very different types of organisations must be reviewed and revitalised, not only with government and regulatory entities, but also with those in the industry's global operation. This includes bodies for the setting of international shipping standards such as the International Maritime Organization, the International Labour Organisation and those directly representing staff and crew interests such as the International Transport Workers Federation. The International Federation and Australian unions representing Australian industry workers, were granted leave to appear in the Inquiry though its terms of reference did not include the impact of events on the welfare and interests of Ruby Princess crew members. This work may already be underway.

Additional critical issues for Carnival Plc include:

How to:

- Develop CV-19 testing for passengers with results obtained before embarkation?
- Develop an onboard capability for CV-19 testing and confirmation of results?
- Provide adequate facilities for the testing and isolation of crew members.
- Integrate and reconcile the requirements of a transportation system with the exceptional customer experience Carnival Plc wish to offer?
- How to deal with any further variations in the virus?

What if:

- Social distancing is required on board because suspect or confirmed cases have been identified? (this may become a regulatory requirement);
- Wearing Masks becomes mandatory on board for all passengers?
- A reduction of the passenger capacity of cruise ships is needed or required by regulation?
- A major redesign of ship infrastructure, cabin design, crew accommodation and work organisation, and ventilation systems is required to minimise the risk of onboard transmission of CV-19?

Cultural Change is the Biggest Challenge for Carnival Plc

It is the work of a leader to create, maintain and improve the culture of a group of people to achieve objectives and continue to do so over time. SLT identifies the tools of leadership, systems, symbols and behaviour needed to make the required cultural shift. Persistence and consistency in using the tools is needed to create new assumptions and beliefs (or mythologies) about the leader and the organisation, what it does, and what it stands for.

Myths are based on actual experience. Myths cannot be changed. Only new mythologies created with persistence and consistency can become more dominant. If there is inconsistency and a lack of persistence, if leaders don't live up to the new standards they espouse, if changes are not consistently applied, the old mythologies spring back and the credibility of leaders and the reputation of the organisation is further damaged, potentially even worse than before.[44]

Of course, what distinguishes a Special Commission of Inquiry, from a standard audit is the publicity and notoriety it attracts. The behaviours and systems exposed are on the public record, prominent in the media for the world to see. The public can read Ruby Princess passenger witness statements at *www.rubyprincessinquiry.nsw.gov.au* An excerpt:

"......*I never heard anything in the safety talk, nor on the whole cruise, about Coronavirus. They always tell you to try and use your own toilet and to sanitise your hands. That's normal on every cruise, I think. There was no more information about health than that....*"[45]

The mythologies, the experience of passengers, cannot be changed. The challenge confronting Carnival Plc is creating new myths and changing its systems including those identified by the SCI. Any changes, SLT posits, are judged positively or negatively against six fundamental human values:

- Honesty,
- Trust,
- Fairness,
- Respect for human dignity,
- Love, and
- Courage

Different social groups may make different judgements against these same values: past passengers, potential passengers (and the families of both groups), ships crews, and other Carnival employees.

This is the cultural transformation journey ahead for Carnival and SLT provides theory and models to help understand how this challenge might be undertaken. The work requires an assessment of how the new system will be placed along the Values Continua through a key step of systems design called the Social Process Analysis.[46]

Systems design work for Government departments and agencies

Two fundamental questions must be confronted to progress managing the risk of a pandemic such as CV-19 through cruise ships. What is the purpose of the national system required, and who is the system owner? Until sorted, the risk of flawed design and implementation remains. Some Critical Issues to consider follow.

How to:

- Decide who will lead this work?
- Decide which minister and portfolio will be the system owner?
- Ensure the systems design work is done at the right level by people capable of managing the work complexity involved?
- Adequately resource the work involved, including providing the necessary authorities to assign work and engage with state agencies and authorities, other stakeholders and relevant expertise?
- Identify and provide the necessary authorities and resources to implement the intent of any policy and system changes?
- Ensure there is a detailed implementation plan?

What if:

- Granting pratique is unsustainable given the level of risk associated with CV-19 (as argued by the SCI with the NSW procedures)?
- The orthodox approach to risk assessment (low, medium, high) is unsustainable given the risks posed by CV-19?
- Departments and agencies argue the required work has already been done or is well underway?
- The economic importance of the industry nationally and at state level is used to argue against tighter regulation?
- Some states but not others resist changes?

Risks of the regulator's 'capture' i.e.. the inappropriate influence exerted on the regulator by the regulated entity - must be considered. Identifying, assessing, and resolving such issues is part of the system design process and addressed in a detailed implementation plan.[47] This includes the training needs identified by the SCI when officials are exercising both federal and state authorities - training to ensure a shared understanding of the context and purpose of the national system.

Conclusions

This case study highlights the policy and systems failures that unfolded in managing the risks associated with the CV-19 virus in the context of the international cruise ship industry. No one will want to see a repetition of what happened with the Ruby Princess, and everybody will expect someone do something about it. The various agencies involved will try to do their best and a great level of energy and commitment will be applied by the people involved. After all, anybody can read the recommendations of the Special Inquiry and somebody will do something...or will something like this happen again?

This is a story ...

...about four people named Everybody, Somebody, Anybody, and Nobody.

*There was an important job to be done and **Everybody** was sure that **Somebody** would do it. **Anybody** could have done it, but **Nobody** did it. **Somebody** got angry about this, because it was **Everybody's** job. **Everybody** thought **Anybody** could do it, but **Nobody** realised that **Everybody** wouldn't do it. It ended up that **Everybody** blamed **Somebody** when **Nobody** did what **Anybody** could have done.*[48]

On 17 August 2020, the Premier of NSW in response to the SCI report stated that Commissioner Walker found mistakes were made by public health officials but she concluded there were no systemic failures to address. Recommendations for NSW were to be implemented and work with the Federal Government on the other recommendations was to begin immediately. No other public statements have been released by the Premier since then. On 30 July 2021, when approached by the writer for any further information advice or information by or on behalf of the Premier, her Parliamentary Secretary, Ray Williams MP replied:

"In August 2020, the Premier gave a comprehensive response to the report to the Special Commission of Inquiry into the Ruby Princess. Thank you for writing."

Given the limited authority the NSW Government actually has over the national policy and system, this response perhaps was inevitable.

However, this case study has demonstrated the flaws in the design of both the state and federal systems and without actions to address these systemic flaws, the risks will continue. The key issues to be addressed are:

- The lack of clarity on which national agency should have the authority to design/redesign and direct the implementation of what was initially described as a national border protection policy and system;
- The demonstrated underestimation of the complexity of work involved in the design of systems that must operate simultaneously, in an integrated way across different knowledge fields, jurisdictions and locations;
- The lack of shared understanding of the purpose of the overall system with different agencies focusing on various outcomes such

as biosecurity, national security, customs and excise and public health;[49] and

- Because of the confusion around authority, a lack of accountability of a single agency to take the initiative to lead the remedial work required and subsequent risk of on-going inaction.

The risk of inaction looms large. The initiator of the Special Commission of Inquiry, the NSW Premier, sees no systemic issues which is hardly a call to action to other federal and state authorities.

The most likely impetus for systemic change will come from the economic necessity for cruise ship operators to restore consumer confidence in the sector by developing robust screening procedures of passengers prior to embarkation and onboard testing capability.

Nonetheless the international cruise operations in Australia remain suspended with a further review scheduled in September 2021.The emergence of the Delta variant, said to be 5 times more infectious, raises even more challenges to be addressed before operations can be safely resumed.

Progress on the development of a vaccine have been unprecedented with the UK, USA, China and Russia (49) moving from the early stages of development, to clinical trials and regulatory approval of vaccines. Vaccination is now well-advanced in the USA and UK but is lagging in Australia. It can be anticipated that vaccination of cruise ship employees and intending passengers will required. The task for the regulator in this context could simply be to specify this requirement and for a potential cruise ship operator to demonstrate their capability for onboard testing and confirmation of results to an independent assessor prior to authorising a resumption of operations. The grant of pratique, however, would need to be dependent on independent verification of onboard testing to confirm there are no positive CV-19 cases.

There can be little doubt that the Special Inquiry led by Commissioner Walker SC has made a valuable contribution to understanding the public health policy failures associated with the Ruby Princess.

However, from a SLT perspective, the same systemic problems with the management of the CV-19 risks in the cruise ship industry limit the depth of analysis required of the complex national system involved.

The SCI was commissioned by an important but part player in the national system. It did not have the authority to examine federal department key decision makers and there is no requirement on or accountability for these authorities to act on recommendations made.

The Inquiry identified systemic issues, especially relating to the standing assumption favouring the grant of pratique and the possibility that any passenger ship could be assessed as low risk in the light of the substantial public health risks associated with the CV-19 pandemic.

The relevance and additional analytical insights arising from a systems leadership theory-based review are not limited to the case of the Ruby Princess. The interim report into Hotel Quarantine arrangements in Victoria raises similar themes. The 20 Questions of system design would have provided a useful check list to assist the systems design and decision making process, especially given the tight time constraints confronting the public servants, other advisers and political decision makers involved.

Attachment 1 – Terms of Reference

On 15 April 2020, the Special Commission of Inquiry into the Ruby Princess was established. The Special Commission will be led by Bret Walker SC.

The letters patent issued by the Governor to Bret Walker SC under the *Special Commissions of Inquiry Act 1983* (NSW) are available at https://www.rubyprincessinquiry.nsw.gov.au/assets/scirp/files/Letters-Patent-Special-Commission-of-Inquiry-into-the-Ruby-Princess.pdf.

The terms of reference for the Special Commission, set out in the letters patent, require the Commissioner to inquire into and report on:

- The knowledge, decisions and actions of Ruby Princess crew, medical staff and the ship operator, Princess Cruises, with respect to cases or potential cases of respiratory infections on the ship.
- The information provided to, communications between, and decisions and actions of Commonwealth and NSW agencies, including the Australian Border Force, the Federal Department of Agriculture, Water and the Environment, NSW Health, the NSW Police Force, NSW Ambulance and the Port Authority of NSW.
- Policies and protocols applied by Princess Cruises and Commonwealth and NSW Government agencies with respect to managing suspected or potential COVID-19 cases.
- Communications by Commonwealth and NSW Government agencies to passengers disembarking the Ruby Princess.
- Any other related matters that the Commissioner considers appropriate.

In conducting the Inquiry, the Commissioner is to have regard to the global COVID-19 pandemic and:

- the departure from Sydney of the Ruby Princess on 8 March 2020;
- the voyage of the Ruby Princess between 8 March and 19 March 2020;
- the docking and disembarkation of the Ruby Princess at Sydney on 19 March 2020; and
- subsequent efforts to diagnose and treat, and to contain the community transmission of COVID-19 by, Ruby Princess passengers.

The Special Commission has been given special powers under Division 2 of Part 3 of the *Special Commissions of Inquiry Act 1983* (NSW) to conduct the Inquiry.

The Commissioner must report to the Premier and the Governor by 14 August 2020.

Attachment 2 - Levels of Work Complexity

I

"Hands on – completing concrete procedural tasks"

II

"Monitoring and diagnosis of operational processes"

III

"Discerning trends to refine existing systems and develop new systems within a single knowledge field"

IV

"Integrating and managing the interactions between a number of systems"

V

"Shaping and managing an organisation within its environment – maintaining the organisations systems and processes so that it is self-sustaining within that environment"

VI

"Shaping the organisation of the future - creating the ethic on a national and international basis that allows entities to function and manages the relationships between entities of a significantly different character"

Attachment 3 - 20 Questions of Systems Design

1. What is the purpose of the system?
2. Who is/should be the owner?
3. Who is/should be the custodian/designer?
4. What is the underlying theory?
5. How is it to be measured?
6. Is it a system of differentiation or equalisation?
7. What are the current 'benefits' of the poor system?
8. What are the boundaries of the system?
9. What are the linkages with other systems?
10. What structural boundaries does it cross?
11. Is the system one of transfer or transformation?
12. Are authorities and accountabilities consistent with role?
13. Are there proper controls built into the system?
14. Is there an effective audit process?
15. Has the social process analysis been done?
16. Is there a fully outlined flowchart?
17. Is there a design plan that addresses the critical issues?
18. Is there full system documentation?
19. What is the implementation plan?
20. What is the final cost of design and implementation?

Attachment 4 - Additional Quotes

1. Context - Federal Court Action

"We say the owner and operator knew of the risks that passengers may contract coronavirus before the ship left and they failed to take steps to ensure their passengers were safe and protected ... People on board the ship trusted Carnival to do the right thing but they were not told about the risk of coronavirus and some paid the ultimate price for it."

Shine Lawyers Press Release, 24 July 2020 [50]

2. Who is the System Owner and Finger Pointing?

"I have no information that says my officers did not acquit their responsibilities under the Customs Act or the Immigration Act...or that they did not consult with officers of the Department of Agriculture, who provided us with information that the New South Wales Health Department had cleared this vessel for disembarkation...(the decision) to allow them off, in relation to the health and biosecurity issue, was one for New South Wales Health."

"I had six officers board that ship. They did their job. I've got no information in front of me other than accusations about we didn't do something right."

Commissioner Outram, Australian Border Force, 25 March 2020 [51]

3. Critical issues raised by NSW Health Department Expert Panel

"...Strongly recommend on public health grounds that all results available for cruise ships where this is the final port for disembarkation for the cruise ships before disembarkation commences. Our experience from the follow up of a much lesser number of negative results daily from the coronavirus clinic has identified: people don't have an Aussie sim so no contact number, numbers can be

wrong or ring through, hotels can get very concerned if people are discharged pending test results. There will also be community expectation in light of the Japan incident. Noted that this may delay disembarkation by a few hours thus delaying the cruise ship timetable, but I know that these delays can be managed by the Ports Authority – especially if they are planned delays. Where it is not the final port this could be relaxed as the passengers will be returning to the ships...”

Dr Leena Gupta, Expert Panel member, email [52]

“Given the Japanese experience it appears that this virus spreads efficiently in this petri-dish environment. Once the horse (should that be the pangolin) has bolted off the vessel, we have lost control (for many of the reasons Leena (Dr Gupta) has given – international mobile phones/vs local SIMS etc).

Thus I strongly suggest that specimens are choppered in to a lab 8 hours before arrival for “flu cases” that are negative on rapid flu testing... I would prefer that people did not disembark if there were any people on board from any country/area with person-to-person transmission and flu-like illness on board until the results are available. ”[53]

Dr Durrheim, Expert Panel member, email

4. Medical assessments advice to cruise companies

“...cruise companies are also requested to consider making medical assessment for ARI/ILI free to passengers as well as crew. Ships not providing free consultations are at greater risk of being considered at risk for COVID-19 as ARI/ILI cases may be less likely to have been identified”. [54]

Enhanced Procedure Guidelines, March 9, 2020

5. Concerning adequate supplies of swabs

“In the circumstance of a growing global health concern (noting that a pandemic had not yet been declared on 8 March when the

Ruby Princess left Sydney) the stocking on board of more swabs than might normally be needed would have been prudent, particularly in light of the enhanced procedures requiring swabs to be taken for COVID-19 testing."[55]

"...genuine attempts were made by Dr von Watzdorf to obtain what she thought would be a sufficient number of swabs for COVID-19 testing..."[56]

Commissioner Bret Walker QC, SCI Report

6. Passenger witness statement

"32 We did get a letter saying that we had to self-isolate from the last port. that it was a government regulation. This meant that we would have to self-isolate for ten days when we got home. I still have that paperwork. Every night you got a newsletter in your cabin and I think it was just stuck in with that. I do not have any recollection of an announcement for people who were sick to go down to the medical centre. That's something that you're always told to do though, on every cruise, that wouldn't have been out of the ordinary.

34 It was a very quick get off. There weren't any health checks or questions about whether you were sick. I did not see anyone with masks and/or gloves on the cruise ship or in disembarking......

43 On Friday, 27 March 2020, I was moved into the same (hospital) room as Karla. Karla was the one that told me I was positive for Coronavirus. I said that I hadn't yet heard...

48 At 2.1 0am on Sunday, 29 March 2020, Karla passed away. She just stopped breathing. I couldn't hear her breath anymore breath. We were only 4 foot apart so I got up to check on her. I held her hand to see if she had a pulse but there was none. I could tell then that she had passed away. I stayed like that, with her, for 10 minutes before I went back to bed where I could still see her. Karla wasn't being monitored, so no-one came into the room until 4.50am. The Nurses put their heads to the window and I waved them in. I know that I could have alerted someone, but I think I was in a bit of shock. I had just watched my wife die and there was nothing I could do"[57]

Bibliography

Systems Leadership - Creating Positive Organisations. Macdonald I, Burke C, Stewart K. 2nd Edition, Routledge, 2018.

Report of the Special Commission of Inquiry into the Ruby Princess. NSW Government, 14 August 2020.

www.rubyprincessinquiry.nsw.gov.au

Tasmanian Department of Health; Interim Report, CV-19 Cases. 29 April 2020.

Media References

ABC Four Corners program, dedicated to the voyage of the Ruby Princess ending on 19 March 2020.

Shine Lawyers Press Release, 24 July 2020.

NSW Premier's Press Conference, 17 August 2020.

Jenny Noyes, Sydney Morning Herald, 30 September 2020 citing Emerging Infectious Diseases Journal, October 2020.

http://www.cruising.org.au/Tenant/C0000003/5677_CLIA_Economic_Impact_Statement_Web.pdf

https://www.abc.net.au/news/2020-07-30/border-force-ruby-princess-coronavirus-test

https://www.carnivalcorp.com/ https://www.carnivalcorp.com.

Notes

[1] In an interim report published 29 April 2020, the Tasmanian Department of Health found the likely original source of the spread of CV-19 is one or both of two inpatients of the hospital who acquired the disease while on the Ruby Princess.

[2] Shine Lawyers Press Release, 24 July 2020 - see Attachment 4

[3] Special Commission of Inquiry Report (SCIR) paras 1.7 – 1.9.

[4] http://www.cruising.org.au/Tenant/C0000003/5677_CLIA_Economic_Impact_Statement_Web.pdf

[5] According to an email exchange, obtained by the ABC under Freedom of Information, the senior Australian Border Force (ABF) officer on board when 2,760 people were allowed to disembark the Ruby Princess cruise ship mistakenly believed passengers displaying "flu-like symptoms" had tested negative to COVID-19, when they had instead tested negative for the common flu. https://www.abc.net.au/news/2020-07-30/border-force-ruby-princess-coronavirus-test-

[6] Premier's Press Conference 17 August 2020.

[7] SCI p 47-49.

[8] Systems Leadership-creating positive organisations. Macdonald, Burke and Stewart. 2nd Edition, 2018. p161-164

[9] Authority is the right of a person, a role incumbent, to lawfully require another person to act in a prescribed way. The authority will be specified in a document or agreement and can be considered a resource expected to be used in the specified circumstances. The effective use of

authority requires good social process skills. See Macdonald, Burke and Stewart; p 89 and p 325-326.

[10] Exhibit 9 Special Commission of Inquiry (SCI)

[11] Systems Leadership 2nd Ed Chapter 9

[12] See Attachment 3. For a detailed discussion of 20 Questions see 2nd Ed: chapter 17.

[13] 2nd Edition p. 238.

[14] SCI Exhibit 119 at para 53.

[15] SCI 14 August at para 11.3

[16] See Attachment 4 and Senate Select Committee on Covid-19

[17] SCI at paras 11.42, 11.43, 11.44 (emphasis added)

[18] Important issues must be considered and resolved when there are linkages with other systems when designing a system of IV complexity. These issues are much easier to resolve when there is clarity about the system owner. See Macdonald et al pp 240-241)

[19] SCI at para 11.12 - see Attachment 4

[20] SCI at para 11.9

[21] Macdonald et al at p 204

[22] SCI at para 5.40 - see Attachment 4

[23] For a discussion of critical issues as part of the 20 Questions of System Design see 2nd Ed. p.245

[24] See discussion of Team Leadership and Team Membership: Macdonald et al Chapter 15

[25] See the discussion of Question 3 Macdonald et al at p.239

[26] SCI NSW Government Submission 13 July 2020 at paras 9-13

[27] SCI at para 1.35 and 11.13

[28] https://www.carnivalcorp.com/

[29] SCI at para12.36

[30] SCI paras 12.7 to 12.15

[31] SCI para 12.31

[32] SIR at para 12.32

[33] ibid para 12.32 - see Attachment 4

[34] SCI para 12.25 - see Attachment 4

[35] SCI at para 12.42

[36 SCI at para12.43

[37] SCI at para 12.42

[38] SCI at para 12.75

[39] For disturbing evidence of these incidents see ABC Four Corners program, dedicated to the voyage of the Ruby Princess ending on 19 March 2020

[40] Macdonald et al at p 241

[41] Macdonald et al at p 243

[42] ABC News 15 August 2020

[43] See Macdonald et al for a discussion of the work of leadership creating a culture and social process analysis in systems design; Chapter 12 and Question 15 on how to design systems at p 243

[44] See chapter 12 Systems Leadsrship 2nd edition

[45] Exhibit 64 SCI - see Attachment 4

[46] Macdonald et al Question 15 of 20 Questions of system design at p. 243- 244

[47] Macdonald et al; p. 245- 246

[48] Unknown author - adaptation of poem by Charles Osgood

[49] The absence of a shared understanding of the purpose of the system was evident in the aftermath of decision to grant pratique when ABF refused to pass on the passenger manifest from the Ruby Princess to Qantas despite repeated requests, citing privacy reasons. The result was further transmission of the virus of some 8 to 11 passengers on a flight to the USA. As late as 30 September 2020 ABF indicated it had not been asked to establish a standing procedure for sharing manifests to airlines from sea vessels. This provides a telling example of the inaction and confusion that arises when there is a lack of clarity of authority about system ownership and no shared understanding of system purpose among the agencies and organisations involved. See Jenny Noyes, Sydney Morning Herald, 30 September 2020 and Emerging Infectious Diseases journal, October 2020

[50 Shine Lawyers Press Release, 24 July 2020

[51] ABF Press Conference, 25 March 2020

[52] SIR at paras 5.24-5.30

[53] SCI at para 5.31

[54] SIR at para12.24

[5 ibid

[56] SCI at para 12.50

[57] Exhibit 64 SCI

3

The UK NHS – the significance of symbols

WRITTEN BY IAN MACDONALD

The National Health Service as sacred: An example of the significance of symbols

(This chapter is based on an article by the author published in the UK Guardian Newspaper 25th April 2020)

The National Health Service (NHS) has been understandably front and centre of attention during this pandemic in the UK. People have been and are showing appreciation in so many different ways; sponsored activities, international concerts, people simply clapping hands or banging saucepans on a Thursday evening. We are perhaps as never before grateful to people who help manage a transition between health and illness and back again, between home and hospital and hopefully back again to our families and so-called normal life.

Societies have always been fascinated by thresholds; the significance of moving from one state to another and of the rituals and symbols that accompany these transitions. Traditions like carrying across the threshold of a doorway in marriage, baptisms, bar mitzvahs, and many other rites of passage to adulthood or academic or professional qualification. Sometimes these thresholds are crossed relatively easily other times less so, for example being locked in prison or "locked down" during this pandemic.

During this pandemic it seems that our boundaries are constantly changing; where we can go, who with, what for. Who has authority to help, advise us, who can tell us? In sociology Arnold von Gennep and Victor Turner wrote about liminal roles. Those who can help and guide us through transition, and of those who can actually live across different worlds and do not obviously belong entirely the one state or another. Durkheim observed and described the difference between the sacred and profane where the sacred refers to "collective representations that are set apart from society, all that which transcends the humdrum of everyday life".

Perhaps the most significant transition, that both fascinates and frightens us is the ultimate one between life and death. Intellectually of course we all know that we are going to die, but the reality of this and how and where this happens is hugely significant and for many terrifying. It has traditionally been the role of religion to help us make sense of this ultimate threshold and to help us across without fear and indeed with some hope. Whether this is the last rights administered by the Catholic priest or the Boatman crossing the river Styx, most societies have developed belief systems, rituals and symbols that can and do play a significant part in containing anxiety and opening up the promise of a better place to come.

Today in a modern, largely secular society many have turned away from religion and priests to play this comforting role in this final transition. However, materialism has not necessarily reduced our anxiety. Indeed, whole industries are built around our fight against ageing and by implication denying or at least delaying the inevitability of death.

We may be even more fearful than ever. We can be made to look younger by surgery, clothing or cosmetics but no one has in fact avoided this final transition, (even Jesus) and we are still in need of people to help us when that reality, or at least the possibility of that reality becomes undeniably apparent.

Working with the NHS over many years I have for some time thought about how the NHS as an institution and its staff as individuals have come to take on, albeit unwittingly the role of religion and priests when it comes to this ultimate transition. As such the NHS has become sacred. Liminality and the sacred are infused with symbolism. There is an assumption that those involved with the sacred have an ability to rise above normal feelings. This is exemplified by symbolic language constantly apply to NHS staff. They are "saints", they are "angels" they perform "miracles", they are perhaps, literally incredible. This goes beyond the ordinary language of appreciation that we might use in relation to other people in service work. The applause and banging of saucepans for the NHS staff was a new but almost required ritual where people might feel guilty if they don't join in. Later more mortal folk such as carers, delivery drivers, postal workers, and teachers were added but everyone acknowledged it was the NHS staff that were on the real frontline; facing danger every day and actually being on the threshold between life and death.

Is this not just appropriate recognition and appreciation? I think it goes beyond that. It is in effect elevating the NHS and its staff to the sacred. My concern about this primarily concerns the NHS staff themselves. Well before the pandemic there had been understandable concern about the well-being of NHS staff and the stress they experience in their work. Now with the pandemic we are putting them under even more stress. The problem I think is one of unconscious identification. After all it is very moving to be appreciated especially after long periods of austerity and lack of recognition. It can also be quite confusing when the very people who have denied pay rises and better conditions join in this public appreciation. Politicians publicly applauding while cutting budgets. Being called a saint or miracle worker might be very complimentary but it may come with price: an unconscious expectation that you really are a saint. Saints endure pain, saints appear to need little or no rest or sustenance. What happens when people do die as they must? The danger is that the personal experience of the staff is one of deep failure and dissonance as so well described in the book: This is Going to Hurt by Adam Kay.

Expectations associated with being part of the sacred and the internalisation of those expectations may actually be unrealistic but at the same time mutually encourage those unrealistic expectations. Medicine is not a religion, getting better is not simply a matter of belief. No matter what the advances in medicine, pandemic or otherwise the NHS and its staff cannot stop us dying even though they can prolong our lives. Of course the NHS staff do, will and always should play a part in managing the transition from life to death, palliative care being a prime example. Many have directly experienced the sensitivity of staff at such a time and their crucial work in managing a good death. However, we must be mindful that staff are human beings and not to idealise. Assaults and abuse of NHS staff has risen significantly in recent years, indicating unrealistic expectations and unreasonable assumptions. We don't want martyrs.

NHS staff should not be under pressure externally or internally to work unsafely whether that be long hours or without appropriate PPE. Leadership in the NHS through courageous management and psychological support should protect frontline staff from this over expectation. Let us rather appreciate staff through better pay and conditions for work, rather than adulation for their miracles. Let us recognise they do have the same feelings as us including confusion, uncertainty, fear and anger. The consequences of elevating NHS staff to the sacred is that we might be in danger of forgetting what is an essential element of religion: forgiveness for being human.

Since this paper was written NHS staff, so praised by Government were offered a 1% pay rise which due to inflation is in real terms a pay cut. After significant outrage this was increased to 3% in July 2021 but most of that has to be found from within existing NHS funding; robbing Peter to pay Paul. Also, at time of writing this has not actually been paid.

Symbolically one of the nurses who treated the Prime Minister in Intensive Care during his Covid illness, Jenny McGee has resigned saying: "We're not getting the respect and now pay that we deserve. I'm just sick of it. So, I've handed in my resignation". Rachel Clarke, a palliative care doctor and writer also gives an account of this dissonant symbolism in her book Breathtaking: Insidethe NHS in a Time of Pandemic. See also Julie Highfield's chapter in this book.

When Systems, Symbols and Behaviour do not align there is a significant detrimental effect on behaviour and morale. Mythologies are created around the Universal Values (e.g. Respect above) and damage is done to people and organisations.

References:

Arnold Van Gennep: Rites of Passage, University of Chicago Press: 1909

Emile Durkheim: The Elementary Forms of Religious Life, Allen and Unwin 1912

Adam Kay: This is Going to Hurt: Picador 2017

Rachel Clarke: Breathtaking: Little Brown Book Group, 2021

A perspective from South Africa

WRITTEN BY HILTON BARNETT

Context

Systems Leadership Theory & Practice has been part of my life for 25 years. My experience is that the principles help to understand social behaviours and work decisions of people in a wide range of contexts –including beyond the organisations where we work. The principles also help identify how things could be different and, very importantly, how one could work towards achieving that.

Over the years our associates have demonstrated this by helping people to apply the principles in their work, in diverse systems and contexts.

The response to Covid-19 has provided some opportunities to illustrate how the models articulate what goes on in decision-making, leadership, culture and systems. This can be helpful to others, more specifically to the people in organisations with whom we work, both currently and in the future.

Purpose

These notes discuss examples of human behaviour in the global context of the Covid-19 pandemic in order to extract helpful insights for people in leadership positions.

Using Symbols to Lead Change

In the early stages of South Africa's highest level of lockdown against the spread of Covid-19, the president, Cyril Ramaphosa, addressed soldiers before they were deployed to help in the community.

The president wore military camouflage uniform, something he has never done. Notably he did not wear any grand, parade uniform, adorned with false medals – in stark contrast to others in third world countries when the military have overreached or even taken over.

He specifically addressed the soldiers directly at an outdoor location, not as a general speech to the nation from the podium.

He told them he was assigning them a task and claimed the authority to do so. This was significant on two fronts:

- the ruling party tradition tends toward much less direct wording, more like an appeal to values, which often leaves a lot open to interpretation
- his authority at the time was weakened due to internal divisions in the party. During the pandemic there have been several data points indicating he was starting to make greater use of the authority he has as president.

In his address he chose his words deliberately saying this was not the time for "skiet en donder" -a term from the Afrikaans language (the language of the previous "Apartheid" government) literally meaning to shoot and assault. It is often used to describe violent films and fairly accurately described the behaviour of the military and police in the Apartheid years.

He spoke in gentle terms making it very clear that this was about looking after the safety of "our people" and not instilling fear.

The president clearly had a specific purpose in mind and his choice of words, clothing and location all worked together to send the message he wanted. This included taking into consideration the beliefs that people (possibly including the soldiers themselves) might hold about this decision. There was already a narrative developing that the government was using the pandemic as an excuse to establish more state control and to interfere in human liberties on a permanent basis.

Systems Leadership refers to these as *Mythologies*:- the stories that are told about what is experienced, explaining what is behind the experience and how this stacks up against core values (fairness, love, dignity, honesty, courage, trust)

Systems Leadership describes the use of *Symbols, Behaviour* and *Systems* by leaders to encourage a positive culture, underpinned by new *mythologies*. Here the president used two of these leadership tools, symbols and behaviour to send a specific message, including being clear about how he did not want it to be and to try to counter the negative mythologies that existed.

Systems Leadership also identifies the need for clear use of language, which is chosen carefully with regard to the purpose and the context. The president did this.

The language of a task assignment changes the engagement to one that implies authority to require something be done, in a certain way, as well as creating the expectation that there will be some form of accountability.

This is not a general motivational speech, nor a request or invitation. We have quite often found a move to more vague and "soft" language in organisations which stem from – and add to- confusion around authority and accountability. They sound nicer, but they do not actually help create clarity.

Consistency and Dissonance – The President & The Military Part 2

If people see what they expect to see there will be no change.
Very early on after this deployment of soldiers, incidents of violent and degrading behaviour by the both police officers and soldiers were re-

ported. By just 2 months into the lockdown, 10 people were killed at the hands of law enforcement.

Collins Khosa died after soldiers entered his home and beat him with a rifle after seeing in his yard a cup of what they said was alcohol, sales of which were banned during that stage of lockdown (but not consumption at home). His name has since appeared on banners alongside American George Floyd in local protests.

The military did not wait for the courts, instead finding in favour of the soldiers in their in-house inquiry. The Minister of Defence opposed the suspension of the soldiers.

The Minister of police has appeared unmoved. ("General" Bheki Cele was dismissed as national police chief in June, 2012, over corruption charges, but is now the Minister of Police!)

"South Africa's Police Minister Bheki Cele criticized the ruling African National Congress (ANC) party's Black Friday anti-racism campaign, saying it gave criminals an opportunity to turn society against police, local media reported Thursday.

"In South Africa there is no police brutality." He said.

The history of this country, from the dark days of Apartheid through to the current day – and including the 34 people murdered by police during a strike in 2012, is full of brutality.

More than 42,000 complaints were made about the police between 2012 and 2019, including rape, killings, and torture, according to the Independent Police Investigative Directorate.

In all of this the only response from the President has been that soldiers were "over enthusiastic" in their behaviour.

So, despite the initial leadership work of the president, some soldiers did not get the message.

This happens often when leaders are trying to drive change. Managers and others in the organisation might for various reasons think this is just a show and not really requiring that they change their behaviour. This is often supported by the many "change initiatives" and new corporate values, policies etc that they have experienced leading to nothing over the years.

Work is about turning intention into reality.

The President appeared in this instant to be intentionally attempting to drive different behaviour. This view is backed by the way he has spoken on other occasions.

Consistency is an essential part of driving culture. Consistency in individual Leadership behaviour, including their words, and also across all leaders. Culture is not changed by one speech and it is to be expected that behaviours will not change immediately.

This point is well made by Craig Bailie in Daily Maverick, in an article I found whilst following up the Collins Khosa case just before publication of this book. He writes about culture:

"'The way we do things around here'

Culture is best defined in behavioural terms: "This is how we do things around here." Research shows that if organisational culture is prioritised and shaped accordingly, the desired organisational performance will follow."

He goes on to say:

"The SANDF did not possess, and will not possess for some time, the kind of organisational culture necessary to fulfil the expectations that President Cyril Ramaphosa set before it on the eve of its deployment against Covid-19,.."

"....... his (the president) attempt at creating a rhetorical bulwark against the SANDF's outdated military culture before ordering troops to "go out and execute this mission with great success" was too little, too late. Cultural transformation can be a long-term endeavour that requires resources and commitment."[1]

When there were serious breaches of his stated approach, he failed to act in a manner that would support the new culture he was trying to create. His two ministers also failed, and he did nothing visible to address this. Instead, his throwaway line about over-enthusiasm is a powerful **symbol** in the face of violent deaths, reminiscent of the apartheid government's comments.

A key driver of change is **dissonance**. If what happens is what people expect to happen, then why would they change? Something different has to happen and it did not in this case.

A great opportunity for dissonance was missed. The response by the President and his ministers could have sent a strong message to soldiers and policemen, as well as to the public. Instead, his lack of response to behaviour that contradicted his stated intent, confirmed existing mythologies such as:

"There is no accountability in this government – people can do what they like and get away with it"

"You cannot trust their good words"

"The police and the army are still not to be trusted and are allowed to treat us unfairly and without dignity"

"You see, we were right, they are going to bring in more oppression"

"No rich people were beaten up"

"We can abuse our uniform and get away with it"

"The president is too cowardly to stand up to his Ministers"

The result of this is that the good intentions actually cement the culture you are trying to change as they are left hanging with no impact at the very moment they are tested.

Actions, words, symbols and systems need to be consistent and deviations require overt and courageous attention as they provide opportunities to reaffirm the new mythologies.

Getting Better

The above piece notwithstanding, here are two short examples of a more productive response.

President Cyril Ramaphosa suspended one of his ministers for two months, including one unpaid, after she was photographed having lunch with a friend in violation of a strict national lockdown to contain the coronavirus. The Minister of Communications was summoned to explain herself and the president publicly stated:

"Members of the National Executive carry a special responsibility in setting an example to South Africans, who are having to make great sacrifices. None of us should undermine our national effort to save lives."

This action created a great deal of dissonance and the statement about leaders setting an example sent a good message. It is almost unprecedented in this country for this to happen.

More recently the president has also acted in a similar way towards a Minister for abusing state resources and taken a stand on corruption that coincided with arrests and charges of senior government or party members. New mythologies about him are slowly developing.

Similarly, in New Zealand, the Health Minister David Clark was demoted for driving his family to the beach for a walk, in violation of that country's anti-virus measures.

And in Scotland, the Chief Medical Officer resigned after travelling to her second home outside Edinburgh.

And then there is Mr Cummings, then special advisor to the UK Prime Minister, who at the very least broke the spirit of the lockdown by travelling over 400kms for personal reasons whilst knowing he had the virus. His ludicrous comment that he was testing his eyesight was accepted and he has been protected by the Prime Minister with no consideration of the impact of this behaviour as a powerful symbol.

Systems

In Systems Leadership, we recognise the key role systems play as influencers of behaviour, both in the way their design creates limits around what and how things are done, but also in how they are perceived and what *mythologies* they support.

Systems are tools of leadership in driving culture. They are of course ways of organising work and require the right capability in design and implementation to be effective over time and to operate well with other systems across an organisation, or indeed a country.

Therefore a core piece of work is the improving and designing of productive systems, including the work of integrating different systems so that they do not conflict with each other.

When making systems changes, we talk about understanding how these changes might be perceived and predict the responses of the people who will be required to work with them – as key to the success of the change and to sustaining a positive culture.

To do this it is necessary to understand the existing culture and the state of existing systems.

The Covid-19 pandemic required the implementing of new systems. These had to be effective in specific contexts and to work well with each other, and with existing systems.

For example, there were various systems of "Lock-down", prescribed ways of doing business and interacting generally with other people, customers etc; travel protocols; social distancing; the wearing of masks; frequent handwashing and screening.

Later there were procedures for returning to school; doing school work (and other work) on line; testing and tracking and isolating. Various systems for medical treatment and to help people financially were also required.

As things developed more systems were required and some had to be changed either due to new information or through a failure to anticipate impacts and responses to changes made. Some of these changes seemed illogical to many and indeed there were court challenges on that basis. This contributed to the development of mistrust and helped fuel conspiracy theories.

The work on systems therefore needs to consider the issues being addressed in an integrated way and not just focussing on applying rules or procedures to individual issues – which then can cause problems elsewhere.

When changes are required it will be important to understand how these could be perceived and what the resulting behaviour might be. This requires an understanding of the current context, including the circumstances of different groups of people and the prevailing culture.

As we can see, leadership work is complex! This is especially the case when leading a country in times of a global pandemic. Below we look at complexity and then examine context and culture.

Complexity and Capability

In our approach to describing work there is a focus on how work of different *complexity* is required to address the increasingly complex issues as one moves higher up in organisations .

This complexity is inherent in life and we are not referring here to the unnecessarily complicated "noise" sometimes created in organisations. Having people with the capability to both perceive and cope with this complexity is essential.

Covid-19 has given us the opportunity to observe complexity in real time and also how various leaders have handled this. For example:

- Facing a completely new situation, with little experience on how to respond.
- The ongoing interaction between variables: changing scientific knowledge, economic viewpoints and reality, daily changes in statistics, interaction of statistics and culture with behaviour etc
- Having to make wide ranging decisions amidst this uncertainty and change
- Making decisions now, whilst needing to consider how this can be undone later or how it will impact the ability to manage other issues.
- Considering the impact on – and influence from- different entities: eg other countries, various democratic institutions and authorities, national and regional governments.

• Anticipating the behavioural responses

A key part of the work of governments during Covid-19, is therefore to be able to understand the above complexity and to make and implement decisions that take it into account. It is of no use to simply work from a "science" point of view or an "economic" one. At this level there are interactions, 2nd and 3rd order consequences and uncertainty. The work is never "done" and a number of pathways need to be juggled, with different time frames in mind. Decisions are made without having all the data.

The role of the leader in this is to listen to expertise on multiple issues and to make decisions in an integrated fashion, so that the process and outcomes are coherent. A key part of success is having the right capability to do this, as well as being clear of where the authority lies.

Context and Culture

Another key role of leadership is to understand the context, including the existing culture.

We've seen a lot of commentators pointing out what other countries have done and how well it worked there. This can be helpful but caution is advised.

The different cultural and systemic contexts do not make systems easily transferable. The complexity of the situation will often require entirely new approaches.

In addition many of these comments have been premature, not understanding that the consequences of decisions were still unfolding, as is the development of the science and the behaviour of the virus itself. Praise of Sweden's approach is an example.

In South Africa there remains significant inequality in the living conditions, efficacy of basic systems such as water supply, and also in the access to resources through economic status. In this context implementing systems to combat the spread of Covid-19 even if applied equally, will have a very unequal impact. For example:

With little access to water, how does one respond to calls for frequent handwashing?

With crowded living conditions, in some areas in windowless shacks, how does one respond to calls for social distancing and staying indoors?

We saw rich celebrities like Madonna posting from her rose-petal bathtub on social media that this virus was a great leveller and we're all in this together. Recently, as visits to the beach were again banned, a rich South African posted a picture of the beautiful view of the beach, saying how the simple pleasures in life were priceless. The view could be experienced only by someone living in a multi-million Rand house, whilst 'ordinary' people could not experience the joys of the usually free beach.

Protests at the absurdities or unfairness of the restrictions were often by those who were thinking only of their own situation, often privileged. Covid-19 is not so much a leveller as an exposer of the systemic differences still present in South Africa, and the world.

What was also exposed was the massive alcohol problem in the country. Many have complained bitterly about several bans on the sale of alcohol. This was decided in order to free up space in Intensive Care units for severely ill Covid patients. Many thought this was a lie and rather part of some conspiracy, but it soon became apparent from medical personnel that reducing alcohol sales had an almost instant impact on bed availability, and vice versa.

The culture around alcohol and violence, as well as driving drunk was exposed for how bad it really is.

It is often the case that when we start to tackle challenges we uncover other issues. The links between these different issues are often not easily apparent. This further demonstrates the complexity of this work and the need to be looking broadly at a range of interrelated factors – and having the capability to see these links.

2021-Are we getting it Right?

Looking back over 16 months since our first "Lockdown" it is apparent that many of the struggles experienced in South Africa are mirrored elsewhere, even though the contexts are different. Each has had its own complexity including general elections and Brexit. The key issues here have remained the same, with the addition of corruption (our Health Minister has been fired and there are a number of investigations into corrupt PPE dealings). A second addition has been an attempted insurrection, largely driven by those being investigated and charged with corruption.

The President has continued to improve his position partly through the frequent "family meetings" where he has addressed the nation regarding Covid, and partly through consistency and being prepared to make unpopular decisions whilst also engaging with a range of groups and responding to them. His improved position has in turn helped him to start to address competency and corruption in local and regional governments and service provision.

This has not been flawless and there are still inconsistencies between policy, statements and behaviour.

The massive differentiation between rich and poor has been helped by the provision of water to thousands of rural schools, whose lack of water was previously ignored or unknown by officials (their claim). It remains to be seen if the temporary solution will be replaced with a permanent one.

This differentiation has been further addressed through partnerships with the private sector regarding the provision of covid testing facilities as well as vaccination services. The rich still have more options, but some of those have improved for the poor too.

There is differentiation too in business, particularly the mining sector, where mineworkers have continued to go to work in the pit or underground, whilst managers and office staff have worked from home for over a year. This has translated to wealthy people being able to move permanently to their holiday homes at the seaside. Businesses are now needing to deal with more evidence of how some are treated differently to others. This is a complex challenge for the leadership to overcome: how do we act fairly in a situation with such different types of work and living arrangements?

The pandemic has hit the country very hard, one of the worst in the world so far. Much of this has been hidden by the poverty and chronic health problems – many cases are undetected and a lot of people have died with no cause attributed (significant "excess deaths") .

Wealthier people are often unaware of how bad it is and so there are still many who debate the need for such difficult interventions, or even the vaccine. As more people have been getting seriously ill or dying in our "third wave", these views have shifted somewhat.

Perhaps Covid is after all starting to have a "levelling" impact?

What next?

With the huge disparities in living standards and access to basic services being put under the spotlight of the pandemic, the complex work of leadership has to focus ahead to a post-Covid life – if there ever is one.

Key questions arising – "critical issues" in the language of Systems Leadership- would appear to cut across several fronts – as expected with complex work at the level of running a country.

How will the government remove the temporary support that for some people has meant their lives were actually better under the pandemic?

How will the government address the inequalities and generally poor systems in the context of a weak economy and a reduction in tax collection made worse by a big increase in emigration applications?

What if the exposure and prosecution of corrupt officials and party leaders leads to a crisis in government, or worse?

There are plenty more, but let's have a look at these.

Capability:

Our work emphasises the need for getting people with the appropriate capability to do the work – whether it be the ability to perceive and manage complexity or specific skills. There are steps just starting to improve the process of selection, particularly to change the basis from loyalty to merit. This needs to proceed apace.

Mythologies:

- To counteract the predictable beliefs that there is an unfair agenda in the above step, it is important for ordinary citizens, as well as capable government employees to experience the benefits very soon. This will in turn help thwart the attempts to create new mythologies that will help the corrupt regain control of government.

- The country is made up of several cultural groups that experience and interpret government decisions differently. A key piece of work will be to understand how to start to create a unified culture that emphasizes how we are the same, and not how we are different. This is not to suggest a "good news" culture that avoids addressing the real problems, but rather to consider the range of mythologies including those positive ones that perhaps no longer occur along the original divisive lines of race and tribe – and work with systems, symbols and behaviour (the tools of leadership) to encourage these, whilst using the same tools to encourage dissonance around any negative mythologies about dishonesty and unfairness particularly. This adds enormously to the complexity of all the other work.

- The turnaround regarding treatment facilities and availability of vaccines – is already creating dissonance amongst the many who believe this government is neither capable nor willing to serve its people. The charging of corrupt officials and removal of those criminally charged from nomination for office is adding to that dissonance.

- The criminal behaviour – even in dealings regarding health support during the pandemic – seems to be increasing the number of people who judge government corruption as negative against the core values. (yes it is surprising to those who don't know our history that these acts have not always been judged this way)

Systems:

- The internal government systems, including those around structure and authority, selection, performance and procurement – all need to be simplified to enable good work, whilst tightening up on monitoring, auditing and accountability.
- Systems for delivery of services, health education and many others – need to be reviewed and implemented with very clear purpose and a thorough analysis and understanding of how different groups experience them.

The poor existing systems result in only those who have "power" being able to access what they need. This power comes in the form of money to pay for private services (security, transport, medical aid); money to bribe; contacts in the right places; "struggle credentials" (you are looked after because of your role in the fight against apartheid).

In organisations we find that poor systems have the same result: the need for power or special influence to achieve anything, works against merit and opens the door for corruption.

The challenges are huge and only a few are noted here. The principles of Systems Leadership described above help analyse and understand much of what has happened in these months of Covid. They can also help us predict what could be achieved, or could go horribly wrong, depending on the intention and the decisions made to turn these into reality – which is our definition of work.

Notes

[1] Slain by soldiers: Collins Khosa's death and the failure of the SANDF to embrace cultural evolution Craig Bailie, Daily Maverick April 2021

5

Schools and Remote Learning
During the Pandemic

WRITTEN BY CLIVE DIXON

School Education

The people engaged in school education during 2020 reflect on a time when almost everything in their part of the world was transformed. Principals and teachers wrestled with a largely industrial era model of operating to respond to the requirements of governments and the needs of communities in an unpredictable and sometimes volatile environment.

This chapter examines the impact of the Covid 19 Corona Virus on how schools worked during 2020 and the opportunities that have been generated for improving their effectiveness in the future. It is informed by a webinar sponsored by the Systems Leadership Development Association (SLDA) in November 2020, the personal experiences of the author and a number of reports and papers, some of which have been written in response to the events 2020.

The SLDA webinar provides an interesting comparison of the response of schools through the first hand experience of three educators who work in different roles in very different contexts. Ross Linegar is a consultant in New York who is engaged with schools mainly in the Bronx. Peter Linehan is the Principal of Western Cape College located on Cape York in Far North Queensland. Angela O'Brien is a National

Leader of Education, Executive Headteacher and Director of Primary in The Spencer Academies Trust in Derby, England. More information on these people is included at the end of this chapter.

Analysing the response of schools to the impact of the Covid 19 Corona virus through the lens of Systems Leadership, involves identifying and addressing critical issues related to capability, culture, authority and levels of work. This paper does not focus on the broader issue of the political response and its impact on schools, although this inevitably finds a place in the discussion.

The Context

The decisions of governments relating to the Covid 19 Virus determined the response of education systems and schools. Once it was determined that schools would need to change their operations, their main task was to continue to provide effective teaching and learning when all or some of the students could be attending school, completing their studies off site or learning through a combination of both. Even when students attended on site, schools needed to implement the measures required to manage students and staff members safely.

The traditional model of school education, 'face-to-face' learning, relies on students being physically present on site at a school, organised in classes with a teacher supervising, subject to timetables and all the typical systems and structures. 'Remote learning' is the term often used to describe the situation where students complete their studies off the school site, usually at home.

In countries like Australia there has always been a need for 'distance education' for students with medical issues and those that are highly mobile or living in remote areas. Distance education developed over time from envelopes filled with hard copies of readings and exercises being posted back and forwards between the school and student's home, to lessons conducted over short wave radio and more recently to online, real time learning via the internet. In each of these models, students need the support of a capable adult, usually a parent and sometimes a paid tutor.

During the Covid 19 lockdown, a hybrid model of teaching and learning developed when only some students could attend school. In Australian states and many other places, these were the children of emergency workers. With not all students in attendance, those remaining at school were combined in classes to free some teachers to prepare learning resources and teach lessons online. This could mean that in both cases students were not taught by their usual class teacher.

The author of this chapter had direct experience of remote learning when two granddaughters, Sienna and Scarlett, came to stay for two weeks during the lockdown. Sienna is a secondary student. She followed a timetable that included regular, scheduled lessons with her class teacher using a video platform and self-directed lessons organised in units of work accessed online. The work was interesting, structured and appropriate for a student in that year level. Completed work was marked and feedback provided quickly to the student by email. Sienna organised her day to ensure she had completed the work required but she was also aware that in doing so she was determining the 'free' time she had available outside of her studies.

Scarlett, who is enrolled in primary school, completed lessons from units of work provided by the school online. Her class took part in a video meeting each week with their class teacher for what seemed to be a 'check in' as to how they were going and solve problems which had arisen. The lessons were interesting, structured and what could be expected for that year level. Through the units of work Scarlett accessed some very interesting, high quality resources. While grandma, who is currently a teacher, indicated these were commonly used in her classes, granddad, who hasn't taught in the classroom for 25 years, was mightily impressed with the quality and interactive nature of the online resources.

Both girls were required to login by a specified time each morning to be regarded as 'attending" and were engaged in studies for about three to four hours each day. The secondary student required adult assistance with learning for about a third of this time, while the primary student required assistance for most of the time. Assistance was mostly required when new topics were encountered. Both students needed to have use of a computer and access to the internet. It was evident that the secondary student used the computer regularly in studies in normal lessons at school and in completing homework.

These observations are made in a household where both parents are employed full time in professional roles and continued to work during the lockdown. The girls' mother and both grandparents are trained teachers. Both grandparents were not working during the lockdown and could devote time to supporting the students' learning. Good quality internet access, laptops and tablets were readily available.

In some cases schools provided hard copies of lessons to families where technology was not available. Some parents also asked schools to provide the equipment their children would need to complete the work. This was a major logistical exercise in itself.

In New York, Ross Linegar worked with teachers, parents and students to model teaching and learning through online formats. He noted that for many parents this was their first direct experience of how their children can be taught. Students needed only to log in once a day to record their attendance. After a few weeks it became evident that the novelty of online learning was wearing off for many students so that teachers needed to find more and different formats and applications to keep students engaged. Younger students enrolled in preschool and used to hands on activities had difficulty continuing to work from a screen.

Because the decision to move to remote learning was made on a weekend, students had no opportunity to take their books and equipment home. Equipment and resources had to be found in the home. Ross reported that 88 000 tablets were distributed to students in one week in one school district in New York. In the Bronx, only 10% of students had access to the internet.

Across the globe, student access to technology depends on the wealth of the country and the financial position of the school and family. In some news reports parents and their children were seen sitting around the kitchen table, while in other reports students were dressed in their uniforms behind their laptops, replicating a classroom as best they could, reporting to the form teacher for the first lesson of the day. There were also reports of students not receiving assistance and not engaged in learning.

Western Cape College on Cape York in Queensland has primary, secondary campuses and a residential college in Weipa and a primary campus at Mapoon. During the lockdown, the students who had been enrolled in the residential campus returned to their communities across the Cape, the Torres Strait and the Gulf of Carpentaria and did not return to school for fifteen weeks. A biosecurity zone in Cape York, enacted by the Australian government, further reduced the college's access to students, even those living in Napranum, a community located five kilometres south of Weipa.

The college developed a system for case managing students to support their wellbeing as well as supporting remote learning in very difficult conditions. Peter speaks of 'an unrelenting focus on wellbeing' that was critical for remote learning to be successful. In Napranum this meant seeking an exemption from government for teachers to travel to the community. A system was developed whereby the school sent a text to the families to let them know teachers would be visiting the community at a certain time each day. As the school car drove through the community, the children and parents came out on the streets with their devices to access the internet and download their lessons from a mobile hotspot on the dashboard of the school vehicle.

During the pandemic the core purpose of the Spencer Academies Trust in Derby is to educate all pupils at school or at home. Angela O'Brien identified the three critical issues they would need to address to be successful.

What if the curriculum offered isn't suitable for a range of settings?

What if teaching teams do not possess the tools or skills to deliver content?

What if schools don't have the right information at the right time?

The Executive of the Trust used the tools of leadership to address the critical issues and developed strategies in three key areas. Leaders modelled positive behaviour and always put safety at the top of the agenda. While Angela observed that teachers enjoyed adapting their teaching to meet the challenges they faced, school leaders were under a great deal of pressure. The wellbeing of staff members, particularly principals, needed to be addressed.

The Executive developed systems to organise the work they needed to do to support the people working in schools. They summarised the important information that was communicated to school leaders to ensure they received the correct information when they needed it. A simple flowchart of the action to take was developed for principals to use if an active Covid 19 case presented at school. The Executive designed and implemented systems to help principals do their work.

Critical Issues

In Systems Leadership we understand the critical issues to be the 'showstoppers', the issues that if not addressed might stop the work from happening and the purpose being achieved. In identifying the critical issues as 'what ifs' and then determining how to address them as 'how tos' we begin to understand the work we need to do.

For the purpose of this discussion three critical issues are identified.

What if the principals of schools and the leaders of regions and districts do not have the authority to make decisions required in this situation?

What if the wellbeing of staff, student and parents deteriorates during the pandemic?

What if the people do not have the capability to deliver teaching and learning using remote delivery technology?

The work of schools

In most school systems there is a central administration and a district or regional administration that provides supervision of principals and/or support to schools. There has been a trend for authorities to be transferred from the higher levels of school systems to schools. More often than not this is seen as delegation and the purpose is to provide schools with 'greater autonomy'. Delegation often results in the work previously done at higher levels being given to schools, leading to increased workload for people in schools with only small gains in their ability to make decisions.

At the heart of the problem is the reality that autonomy is an impossibility. It is best not to give principals and other people in schools more work to do unless it allows them to be more effective in achieving their purpose. Instead, we should make sure they have the authorities they require to make the decisions required for them to work effectively.

Crises tend to highlight the systems that in normal circumstances are functional but under pressure don't allow people to respond as they need to. Ross in New York and Peter in Queensland both provided examples of where principals needed the authority to respond in real time to the circumstances as they developed. Angela outlined how the Spencer Academies Trust Executive used their authority to support principals to do the work required in unusual circumstances.

The role of the central administration is to provide policy so that principals understand the broader context in which they work and have guidelines for what is required. The circumstances in which schools operated changed quickly during the pandemic and principals made decisions which only they could make. In addition, many of the decisions they made during 2020 related to circumstances peculiar to their school; decisions that couldn't be made by anyone external to the school.

The relationship between schools and higher levels of administration changed to reflect what was required in a critical situation and in doing so identified what would be most productive in any circumstance. Regional and central administrations began to respond to what principals needed to enable them to make decisions to do what was required. As Ross said on the webinar, 'the situation was reversed and the system started to work bottom up instead of top down'.

This leads to a consideration of the implications of the level of complexity of a role. Complexity increases as the number of variables to be considered increases and there is greater interaction between those variables. Difficult situations help to illustrate the extent of the variables that need to be taken into account and the authorities a principal needs to make decisions in the work of their role.

In turn, if these are the decisions a principal should make and these are the authorities the principal will require, then what are the authorities of the regional and central education administration and how does each level relate to the others. The levels of work are more than a framework for supervision or 'line management'. The relationship between one level of work and the next is based on mutuality. It should be the work of central and district administrators to create systems that help the people in schools do their work.

Angela provided us with a glimpse of what this might look like through the leadership of the Spencer Academies Trust in Derby. The government throws problems at schools, so in addition to providing teaching and learning, schools are expected to provide medical advice, feed students at school and now at home. Schools become the first point of call when there's a problem, if for no other reason than schools have direct contact with students and families. This is a familiar problem in school systems across the world.

The Trust Executive uses the Tools of Leadership - symbols, systems and behaviours - to help principals to do their work. In a fast changing environment, where governments sometimes issue directives in the middle of the night to be acted upon the next day, the Executive ensures that communications are summarised so that principals receive the information they need, when they need it.

The opportunity exists to use the pandemic response to understand what schools need to be effective and determine what it is that districts, regions and central administrations should do to help schools do the work they need to do to achieve their purpose. Instead of whimsical notions of autonomy, give principals the authorities they should have had available to them then and now, to make the decisions they need to make.

The Queensland Association of State School Principals has released a White Paper, 'Reimagining Education in Queensland's State Primary Schools'. Described as a new narrative, the White Paper intends to begin a conversation about the future of primary school education in Queensland and more broadly.

'A different story of schooling might allow us to deliver the outcomes we say we want for all our students. School leaders would have the flexibility to meet the unique needs of their communities, the necessary resources to effect equity, the agility to shape changing circumstances, and the space to nurture the mindsets that prepare all learners – leaders, teachers and students – to engage and be curious, as we create a meaningful future together.' (p2)

The paper was not written directly in response to the circumstances of 2020. However, as is often the case, the issues that are most prominent in critical situations may have been there all the time. People have put up with them, worked around them or found alternative, unauthorised but none the less effective ways of doing their work. The ongoing story is about school leaders having the authority, capability and resources to develop the partnership of leaders, teachers and students to focus on learning as a means of creating the future.

Well-being

Our three webinar presenters spoke of the need to address the issue of wellbeing, not just relating to staff members and students but also to parents and caregivers who are now directly involved in their children's learning. While implementing programs to promote wellbeing can make an important contribution, it is no surprise that the way an organisation operates has a significant impact on the lives of the people who work there.

Parental engagement is typically a school strategy that is enacted on the school's terms as one-sided, transactional events. There are limited opportunities for direct involvement in children's learning with parents mostly playing passive roles except in extra curricula activities, fundraising and working bees. The relationship between teachers, parents and students can too easily become a contest because there is not a common understanding of the purpose of school education or of the roles that the people play.

Remote learning requires schools to understand and recognise the contribution that students and parents make. It must have a clear purpose and teachers, parents and students must have an informed understanding of each other's role. Schools can develop systems to help teachers, students and parents to contribute to the student's learning. This is an alternative course of action to propping up a traditional model of school education and dealing with the negative behaviours it can drive in all participants.

Angela spoke of using symbols, systems and behaviours to create a culture of togetherness in Trust schools. The Executive team members modelled and led the development of what she describes as *a positive, collective energy* to contribute to the wellbeing of students, staff and parents. The work of the Trust executive has resulted in a recognition of the contribution that schools can make to the lives of students and families.

In Australia, the Grattan Institute has recommended that government provides schools with additional resources to address the wellbeing needs of students as they return to school. They recognise that the well-being of students affects learning and recommend trialling the use of two initiatives that have been shown to boost student well-being and learning. The first is teacher training in explicit teaching of social and emotional learning, including teaching broader life skills such as how to self-regulate emotions. The second initiative is targeted behaviour support.

Training classroom teachers in the explicit teaching of social and emotional learning would strengthen the relationships between students and between teachers and students. Grattan argues that targeted behaviour support is best undertaken by trained specialists over a longer time frame.

The response to the pandemic helps us understand what is important in how we operate our schools and how this affects the well-being of the people who work in them. Changes in how schools work combined with the implementation of specialised programs in all year levels from preschool to secondary school provide an opportunity to address the issue of well-being for students and staff members.

Blended Learning

The message from our presenters is that the roles of the various players changed significantly with the introduction of large scale remote learning. The adage 'systems drive behaviour' comes to mind.

When a teacher is solely responsible for a class of students, it leads to them being isolated from colleagues, school leaders and parents. The traditional system of classroom teaching drives privatisation of practice. On the other hand, remote learning requires teachers, parents and students to work together in the student's learning. Each party has a role to play and each is dependent on the others. Peter identified a mythology broadly held by teachers and principals, described in his words, 'We need to get over our *preciousness* of believing that students have to be in the room with us for there to be effective teaching and learning'.

In the webinar we discussed a model of 'blended learning', using information technology more than we currently do, in conjunction with face-to-face learning to achieve a synergy that is more than just the best of both worlds.

Our presenters talked about the lengths that some students go to in order to complete studies at home. In poor families students may have accessed online studies through a smart phone because that was the only device available. In the Bronx teachers noticed the number of primary age students who were accessing their work online late at night. They found that because the younger ones were down the pecking order, they accessed a device after adults and older students had finished for the day.

Ross Linegar suggests that remote learning 'empowers' the people involved. Students can put forward their own ideas on what they need and how they can best learn. Parents can observe their children being taught by teachers and can observe what good teaching looks like. They find out how they can use materials in their homes and use their understanding of their children and their own skills in teaching their children. Parents contribute directly to their child's learning. Teachers bring expert knowledge and skill to the partnership but depend on the parent and student for their input for the process to be successful.

In addressing the critical issue, *What if the people do not have the capability to deliver teaching and learning using remote delivery technology?* it became evident that younger teachers had more capability to use the technology required in remote learning. A mythology that we should always go to the experienced teachers because they know all there is to know about teaching was challenged. Roles were reversed and it was younger, less experienced teachers coaching the experienced teachers how to teach using information and communication technology.

The elements of the Systems Leadership model of capability include Technical Skills, Knowledge, Social Process Skills, Mental Processing Ability and Application. A broad implementation of remote learning requires ongoing development of capability in using technology. In this teaching old dogs new tricks scenario, the good news is that it is possible to teach the required technical skills to teachers, teaching assistants and other school support staff.

The greatest opportunity lies in what we can do for students. Since the 1970s educators have talked about catering for the individual needs of students and have tried many different ways of doing this with limited success. Relying on support staff to deliver specific learning programs to individual or small groups of students can separate students from the class program and their peers. Support staff providing classroom teachers with strategies and additional resources to use with the student in the classroom can add to their workload and doesn't provide any additional time. While much of the focus has been typically on learning deficits there is an increasing emphasis on meeting the needs of very capable students in areas across the curriculum.

In recent years the term 'individualised learning' has morphed into 'personalised learning' which means tailoring a student's learning to match their learning needs but also seems to include a broader focus on developing the student's interests and talents. An OECD 2012 background report for the International Summit on the Teaching Profession discussing preparing teachers and school leaders for twenty first century education said:

"the goal of the past was standardization and conformity, today it is about being ingenious, about personalising educational experiences; the past was curriculum centred, the present is learner centred, which means that education systems increasingly need to identify how individuals learn differently and foster new forms of educational provision that take learning to the learner and allow individuals to learn in the ways that are most conducive to their progress." (p12)

Online learning is used extensively in tertiary education. While the benefits are often seen in terms of reduced costs and in some cases has led to student dissatisfaction, it can afford students greater flexibility to study where and when they choose. Students can maintain a fulltime job and live anywhere and complete studies.

The age and developmental stage of the student is important in considering the use of online learning in school education. Preschool and primary school age children require more interaction with teachers and other students in learning, for socialisation and supervision for health and safety reasons. Some activities could not occur without a number of them being involved. Students with special needs require additional individual and small group support. During the lockdown, students with disabilities generally continued to attend school for face-to-face learning.

Some enterprising schools and private businesses working in this area have developed learning programs using technology that provide teachers, parents and students with lessons, assessment and real time feedback on progress. These programs allow the teacher and student to focus on what the student needs to learn during class time when learning is face-to-face and provides the students and teachers with the ability to accelerate learning or to study areas of interest at any time of the day, at school or at home.

For more information on a system designed for this purpose see the addendum "Atherton State High School - The School Learning Management System'.

Conclusion

The response of schools to the pandemic has highlighted existing shortcomings in the operations of school education and also revealed opportunities for improving the work of schools in the future. At this point in early 2021, people in general and specifically in schools speak of getting back to normal. While it may be natural to feel this way, it is hoped that the opportunities for change for the better are not lost.

In discussions with parents, teachers and school leaders following the lockdown, the current author was surprised at the difference in responses. School Leaders generally saw there will be a return to the traditional model of face to face, on site learning and had not continued to develop their schools' online presence. Teachers spoke of the difficulty with the rushed introduction of remote learning and recognised that the different levels of student engagement in learning depended on access to technology and support in the home. They generally believed that making the learning activities and resources available online would be beneficial to student learning and engagement. Students could access materials whenever they needed or wanted to and parent support would be worthwhile wherever it could occur, even if not at the previous level when parents were isolated at home. The parents who had engaged with their children's learning recognised they would not be able to devote the time they did under lockdown conditions but believed it was beneficial for students to access materials online outside of class time. They also indicated they would value continuing communication with the school through social media and with the child's teachers using email and video platforms. While it had to happen this way during the pandemic, it would be good to continue when things returned to 'normal'.

Students viewed blended learning optimistically. They enjoyed the flexibility that the online learning component provided but also looked forward to engaging with their teachers and classmates. Perhaps they best see that blended learning can bring together the focus of face-to-face teaching, the social, emotional and developmental aspects of student learning with the structured programming, flexibility of time and place of through online learning. If blended learning is to become a reality and benefit student learning, a number of factors will need to be addressed.

1. The capability of teachers, teaching assistants and parents to use information and communication technology in teaching and learning should be developed as technology is rolled out.
2. Governments should scale up the development of the most effective online learning programs that have been developed by private businesses and schools and ensure they meet the qualities required in the delivery of blended learning to school age students.
3. Resourcing allocations to schools should be reviewed to ensure that every student is able to access the technology required to engage in blended learning.
4. Curriculum should be developed to meet the needs of 21st century learning and be provided to teachers in a form that helps them in their teaching and facilitates blended learning.

5. The capability of teachers should be developed to provide social and emotional learning.

6. Specialists should be provided to all schools to provide intensive long-term interventions for students with behavioural needs.

Finally, and perhaps the most important opportunity available to us, is to revisit what it is that principals and teachers need to operate effectively in the twenty first century. If the one size fits all methodology isn't suitable for student learning, then it's also not an appropriate way to organise the work of schools.

It's time to understand the work that needs to be done in schools and the levels of complexity that are involved. Pay rises are necessary and arguments over resourcing levels and conditions will continue, but at the heart of the matter is the need for schools to have a clear purpose and for principals and teachers to have the authorities they need to do the work required to achieve that purpose.

Bibliography

OECD. (2012) *Preparing Teachers and Developing School Leaders for the 21ˢᵗ Century: Lessons from around the world.*

Queensland Association of State School Principals (2020) *Reimagining Education in Queensland's State Primary Schools.*

Sonnemann, J. and Goss, P. (2020) *Covid catch-up: helping disadvantaged students close the equity gap.* Grattan Institute.

Systems Leadership Development Association (2020) *School Education Webinar https://youtu.be/qC_ccD8TTE8.*

Addendum 1

Presenters to the Systems Leadership Development Association WEBINAR November 2020.

Ross Linegar has worked in education for 42 years as a teacher, a principal of several schools in Queensland and as a consultant to school districts and states, specialising in developing principal leadership. He is currently working with school and district teams in New York, mainly in the Bronx and Queens.

Peter Linnehan is the Principal of the Prep to Year 12 Western Cape College located on Cape York in Far North Queensland. The college has a primary campus, secondary campus and residential college located in Weipa and a primary campus at Mapoon. Peter has extensive experience working in Queensland state education, independent schools, international schools and most recently in the Indigenous Education Branch based in the Queensland Department of Education central office.

Angela O'Brien is a National Leader of Education, Executive Head-teacher and Director of Primary in The Spencer Academies Trust in England. Many of the 14 primary schools in the Trust serve disadvantaged communities including Wyndham Primary Academy, an outstanding school which has been awarded EEF Research School status. In the New Year's Honour list Angela was awarded an Officer of The Order of the British Empire in recognition of her services to education.

Addendum 2

Atherton State High School - School Learning Management System

At Atherton State High School, an enterprising teacher by the name of David Platz developed an excellent online learning system that can be used for all levels of education. Since 2010, the School Learning Management System (SLMS) has demonstrated the capability to liberate the learning potential of students and contribute significantly to addressing issues of teacher well-being.

The Purpose of the School Learning Management System is to provide a universal online 'flipped classroom' learning solution for all students, that solves specialist teacher shortages in regional, rural and remote schools, so that no Australian student is precluded from pursuing tertiary studies requiring STEM and other advanced pre-requisite courses.

The School Learning Management System is committed to:

1. Reversing Australia's declining performance in education
2. Demonstrating innovative 21st century education delivery methods
3. Re-inventing a new interactive eLearning experience for students
4. Facilitating new and innovative multi-learning pathways
5. Providing seamless transitions between education sectors for staff and students (primary, secondary, tertiary, international)
6. Developing teacher capability in 21st century pedagogy and andragogy using 21st century learning management systems
7. Replacing disengagement of highly capable and other 'at risk' students with enthusiastic discovery learning.

Features of the School Learning Management System

1. A learning system for teachers and all students that contains all of the required resources for all courses, subjects, units of work and lessons.
2. Videoconferencing with the highest levels of student security and safety .
3. A server with robust levels of storage, student security and safety.
4. A new cost effective system for Australian education systems and all schools to improve their performance and contribute significantly to address a range of national education goals
5. A system to improve the performance of non-Indigenous and Aboriginal and Torres Strait Islander students in rural and remote primary and high schools by:
   1. Increasing the quality and consistency of the curriculum.
   2. Significantly reducing the impact of the high turnover of teachers, principals and specialists and the relative inexperience of teachers in these schools.
   3. Offering subjects not readily available in these areas such as physics, chemistry and Specialist Maths etc.
6. Eliminates or minimizes a considerable amount of variation/waste from the day to day operations of a school, from the lives of their teachers and principals.
7. Provides staff and students with access to SLMS 24 hours a day, 7 days a week, 52 weeks a year, anywhere that the internet is available
8. Lessons can be downloaded as required.

* * *

6

A UK Intensive Care Unit in the Pandemic

WRITTEN BY DR JULIE HIGHFIELD

Throughout this volume, Systems Leadership (Macdonald, 2018) has been presented as a coherent approach to understanding organisational contexts, and in the context of the 2020-21 Covid-19 pandemic. One of the most complex organisations central to the UK pandemic response has been the National Health Service (NHS), and specifically the "frontline". In this chapter we consider one element of the frontline NHS: the intensive care unit (ICU).

Most people infected with coronavirus have a mild to moderate influenza-like illness and do not require hospitalisation or intensive care. However, the figures vary across the globe, suggesting potential differing approaches as well as populations. For example, United Kingdom figures suggest 20% are unwell enough to become hospitalized with Covid-19, with 5% needing admission to an ICU although data from the United States suggests a different picture, with 12% of patients are hospitalised, and approximately one quarter of which were admitted to intensive care (Center for Diseases Control, 2020). In China, of the 55% of patients experiencing respiratory distress, approximately half needed intensive care, and half of those required invasive ventilation (Wang, 2020).

Within Systems Leadership are theories of Capability and Culture, where capability refers to the ability to cope with complexity of work and culture is the formation of coherent social groups. The NHS has multiple layers and systems with complex work and different subgroups and cultures. *What is the work of an ICU?* Put simply, in intensive care the work is to offer life sustaining treatment to a patient who has failure in one or more of their vital organs; it offers the patient time . The work is carried out utilising a high ratio of staffing; with standards indicating one or two nurses to a patient, and one doctor to every eight patients (GPICS, 2019). In the Covid-19 pandemic, there were many patients who required admission into the ICU, with UK estimates from January 2021 (the "second wave") estimating an additional 2251 patients in an ICU bed against a baseline in January 2020 of approximately 3848- and surge to 158% capacity; range 117-210% (Intensive Care Society, 2021). This surge in capacity has required a planned, sustained and co-ordinated approach to space, staffing, and equipment.

System Design: Capacity Planning and Preparation

In Systems Leadership, work is turning intention into reality. Policies are a statement of intent and systems turn that intent into reality. To manage the healthcare response in a pandemic, preparation should take into account the whole hospital as a system and involve all levels from hospital to government with clear communication and regional coordination (Dichter, 2014). This integrated system should have the capability to monitor patterns of infectious disease, predict demand, and create the capacity to surge.

This is not the first time the world has experienced a pandemic and learning from the 2003 severe acute respiratory syndrome coronavirus (SARS-CoV) outbreak indicated how quickly critical care capacity was stretched in countries such as Canada (Low, 2004). Following the 2009 H1N1 influenza pandemic, the International Health Regulations committee concluded that "*the world is ill-prepared to respond to a severe in-*

fluenza pandemic or to any similarly global, sustained, and threatening public-health emergency" (Page 128, World Health Organization, 2011).

UK hospital infrastructure was sub-standard to manage the risk of infection spreading due to the lack of negative pressure rooms for individual patients to contain the virus; most UK ICUs still have open bays which were last updated years ago. There was also a lack of ventilators, treacheostomy tubes and shortfalls in medications. Many hospitals did not have sufficient equipment to deliver oxygen at the high flow rates required for Covid-19 patients.

In the UK, there are Guidelines for the Provision of Intensive Care Services (GPICS V2, 2019), which were updated in June 2019 and are endorsed across all the UK intensive care organisations. These guidelines state that units must have documented escalation plans, which must differentiate between escalation during 'normal' operation and escalation during major incidents or pandemic scenarios. Intensive care bed capacity varies across Europe, with an average of 11.5 beds per 100,000 population, but with wide variation; the range is Germany 29.2 and Portugal 4.2, with the UK sitting at 6.6 (Rhodes, 2012). With the UK starting from a lower intensive care bed capacity, its ability to surge under pandemic conditions is inevitably limited.

An important oversimplification throughout the pandemic has been an assumption concerning the creation of additional critical care beds for the surge or "wave" of patients. UK figures reported additional capacity to admit critically unwell patients, however what was not fully appreciated is that there was poor ability to staff those beds with trained intensive care staff. The number of specialist trained ICU staff did not increase, but were instead stretched thinly. Staff were redeployed (such as from paediatric intensive care, operating theatres, paramedics etc) as support, with often quite junior ICU nurses being in supervisory roles. Some of these staff reported the chaos of the first wave, and how poorly their redeployment was managed. In the chaos we lost an opportunity for training a potential "reserve workforce".

In the first wave, this approach to "rob Peter to pay Paul" was deemed acceptable as a short-term solution. However, as it became apparent that the pandemic would not be as short lived as everyone had hoped, this approach could not be continued as other services and patients would be likely to suffer as a consequence. From December 2020 onwards, many intensive care units reported the hospital approach was to wait until the last minute to put non-time critical (elective) surgery on hold and free up staff for a second redeployment. The already exhausted intensive care teams expressed resentment at the way in which they had been treated, many choosing to leave in anticipation that working conditions would be unlikely to improve. Local clinical leaders were reported to have implored their Trust operational management to plan more effectively and not gamble with their staffing levels. At the time of completing this chapter, we head into the third wave: there is discrepancy across the UK in the level of surge required in intensive care, with the North of England experiencing higher numbers than most. In this third (or some argue, fourth) wave, the staffing is poorer and the additional help less available. Intensive Care staff often remark that the wider hospital system and themselves are at odds; the smaller numbers but more intensive way of working means that ICU is a high cost high consequence environment. This is an example of not appreciating the significance of interaction between systems and the consequential impact. A systems approach would have predicted such outcomes.

One decision by UK government was to create Nightingale or Field Hospitals to deal with potential surge in capacity. It is estimated that £532million was poured into converting stadiums, bringing in the army to organise beds and bays. However it is well documented that these field hospitals were massively underutilised. The most expensive hospital in Birmingham was reported to have not treated any patients at all, and the London field hospital treating only a few hundred despite the capacity for 4000 patients (Carding, 2021). One could comment that such hospitals were based on data predictions of the reasonable worse case scenario, but the discrepancy between the beds required and the capacity provided is so vast. This is another example of systems which work within silos. Perhaps when the UK government saw that China created "hospitals in a week" they copied that system without looking at related systems, or detailed demand. However the predicting systems they had available for the possible surge numbers predicated far greater numbers, and at least the presence of surge hospitals offered some comfort to people.

At the start of the Covid-19 pandemic, the World Health Organization also indicated a global shortage of Personal Protective Equipment (PPE) by 40% (World Health Organisation, 2020) despite the well documented hospital-based transmission to other patients and transmission to healthcare workers a feature of previous outbreaks such as SARS and MERS. At the start of the pandemic the piecemeal coordination and supply of PPE impacted NHS workers. NHS Trusts were in competition with each other for the supply of PPE. Longer-term solutions such as hoods were not accessible by some hospitals until much further down the line as other hospitals had ordered their equipment sooner. For the ICU the shortage of PPE was not the only concern, there were also shortages in drugs and equipment such as ventilators. Again we see a lack of understanding system interaction and the result being to undermine purpose and effectiveness.

Capability of ICU leaders

One element of the capability of leaders is the ability to lead in complex situations. ICU direct leadership usually consists of a medical lead, a nursing lead, and an operational lead or non-clinical manager. NHS systems vary, but there are often layers of management between this level and the hospital executive board. The medical lead is often a short-term rotating post and comes with limited authority over medical colleagues, often resulting in a splintered team. The nursing lead post follows a more traditional hierarchical model, with associated authority. To deal with the pandemic, greater clarity and simplification of approach was required in order to speed up the decision making process. The need to work across areas of the hospital with redeployed teams requires a more empathic and flexible leadership style and hence considerable Social Process Skills; building trust quickly and enabling teams to form rapidly. The NHS Staff Survey 2020 reports that 18.5% of staff were redeployed to work into covid zones. This has varied across hospitals depending upon capability.

The NHS is known for several levels of reporting, and with each level of reporting comes additional bureaucracy. It was noted in the first wave by many that due to the rush to get things done, many of these levels of reporting were temporarily removed, and there was an ability to allow collective and clinical leadership. Instead of chaos, systems were developed well because of clearer authority; with clinical decisions such as when and where to escalate across the hospital, and organising equipment happened relatively smoothly. There were several comments of how the NHS would run if we were able to be clinically driven rather than financially driven. Many staff experienced a newfound joy at work. In the summer after the wave, the grip of higher level management returned, and many clinical leads indicated their dismay at having lost the authority to make decisions, and the reintroduction of unnecessary complexity in decision making. In many ways there was a redoubling of efforts due to trying to recoup excessive spends.

In the first wave, ICUs needed to adapt to create a "suspected" Covid-19 patient area in addition to a confirmed area, while also treating patients who required critical care but had no indication of infection, and many needed to take over other areas within the hospital. This required leadership to span wider areas of the hospital, but also for the ICU leaders to work with the wider hospital system in a more integrated way. For medical leadership, staff were rapidly learning from other units to formulate the right response, and many clinicians found the new learning positive, however dealing with high numbers of patients with a single disease type led to more formulaic medicine.

Intensive Care Culture

The pandemic had a significant impact on the culture and the connectedness of the intensive care. PPE caused significant impediment to communication in clinical areas with communication being minimal and practically focussed, with less social conversation. Staff remained cautious about PPE supply and visiting medical and rehabilitation staff clustered their working days around time in PPE. This led to a perception of "inside" and "outside" the ICU, with many nursing staff expressing a feeling of abandonment.

This led to multiple issues. On a wider basis there was social disintegration and relationships broke down. Staff who spent the majority of their time in the red zones became angry with staff who would come and go, and even with support staff who did not have a role to go into these zones. There was a feeling of who has borne the brunt of the work, who has had the worst experience.

Work became less cohesive and there was a tendency towards silo working. A colleague of mine remarked *"I miss the chance to just run something by people- once I am in the red zone and in PPE that's it, no second chances, no thinking things through. Just do the job with what you have to hand".*

To create more physical distancing, staff took fewer breaks together, losing their time to connect informally. With lock down, the opportunities for staff to come together outside work greatly reduced. Here we see examples of systems developing as a result of the change in context and the negative impact on work and relationships not necessarily appreciated. This is partly because work in this area can understandably over-emphasise the technical while missing the significance of the social.

As the intensive care surged to occupy other areas of the hospital this impacted team communication, with team members dispersed over different areas, but also with time as core staffing were stretched cover the higher number of patients and surge areas, so staff were less likely to see each other. To manage the demand many staff were redeployed from other areas, which brought great support but also diluted the core intensive care team. Some staff also noted the burden of supporting the skills of others whilst maintaining their own workload. Working with new teams, trust was hard to build and familiar faces became unrecognisable in PPE.

Symbols, Systems and Behaviour

The NHS has been right at the centre of the UK government public health approach to the pandemic. In the first wave the slogan "Protect the NHS" was heavily promoted as part of an instruction to encourage people to stay at home. Various war-time analogies emerged, describing the NHS as "heroes" going out to the "frontline". Labelling staff in such a way placed high expectations on what they could achieve, and Ian Macdonald wrote an article for the Guardian Newspaper (reported in another chapter in this book) arguing that this approach allows the general public to avoid thinking about the complex work of healthcare. The weekly applause in "Clap for Carers" allowed the public to feel better for what they did not have to do themselves. Many healthcare staff struggled with it and would have preferred a better way of being rewarded for going above and beyond in personal risks and effort and hours of work. The disconnect between symbolic behaviour, rhetoric and systems is exemplified by the dissonant government pay system, which after all this apparent adulation offered a 1% pay rise in NHS England.

One of the common narratives in the news and research has been the impact of the pandemic on mental health and psychological wellbeing. Within intensive care, there has been a surge to respond with offers of resources and expertise, often from those with no prior or working knowledge of an intensive care unit. Some mental health leaders with powerful networks have asserted with confidence that they know the best course of action to prepare and protect ICU staff from the impacts of the pandemic, releasing data without context. As such, some individuals appear entitled to profit from the impact of the pandemic on

ICU staff, assuming psychological trauma without fully understanding that UK staff work within a chronically underfunded and overstretched ICU system, where many units struggled to meet GPICS standards before the pandemic. This is another example of failing to understand underlying systemic causes and only dealing with symptoms.

Later in 2020, the hero's narrative turned sour, with many NHS staff experiencing personal attacks where some members of the public felt their human rights had been violated by lockdown restrictions. There has been for some an ensuing battleground of denial and blame of others- where the public are blamed for the spread of the virus and therefore overwhelming our hospitals ICUs and the hospitals have been blamed for being unable to cope and suffering from mental health problems due to a lack of resilience.

The NHS England Staff Survey for 2020 indicated that across the NHS in England, 44% of staff report feeling unwell as a result of work related stress- a figure which has continued to rise. The pandemic may have exacerbated work related stress, but we need to be careful not to fall into the narrative that stress is in relation to the pandemic alone. Digging into the detail of the survey, the survey did see higher levels of work-related stress reporterd in staff who had worked in Covid areas, however there was also higher levels of engagement and recommending the Trust as a place to work. The relationship, it would seem, is certainly not linear between the pandemic and work related stress in NHS staff.

In truth, there has been a longer-term systemic failure to have a UK ICU bed-base and staffing sufficient to match other European countries.

Summary

The specific example of managing intensive care during the Covid-19 pandemic shows us windows of possibilities and brilliance, however it also poured water into the cracks that were already there. There has been a lack of integration of systems leading to counterproductive outcomes. There is a need for a better appreciation of the complexity of the work, especially the work of leadership in a system where we need to fuel the aeroplane while it is still in flight. It also highlights the importance of Social Process in creating a culture and providing the core conditions to thrive at work and the right level of support for people.

A recent article in the Guardian from a leading voice in intensive care reminded us of John F Kennedy's 1962 State of the Union Address, "the time to repair the roof is when the sun is shining" (Summers, 2021). Are we able to examine the impact of having low ratio of ICU beds per head of population upon the outcomes of the pandemic in the UK? Can we spend the time working on investing in our critical care staffing and skills, with a sustainable model of staffing and a surge staffing, the ICU "reservists". As we enter into the next potential wave of the pandemic, and a winter in critical care complicated by the potential surge in paediatric critical care due to Respiratory Syncytial Virus (RSV) Infection, it would appear the rains have caught up with us again.

With the endurance the UK, and indeed the World, has faced with several lockdowns, fear, and losses by the time we eventually emerge from this pandemic many are likely to collapse and hope it never happens again. There is a risk people will be too disillusioned and exhausted to learn, not just in how to be better prepared for the next pandemic, but how to learn as intensive care, and how to learn as an NHS system.

History tells us that disasters happen again, such as the First World War which was described as the "war to end all wars", until another war occurred 21 years later.

References

Carding, N. (2021, January). Revealed: Nightingale hospitals to cost half a billion pounds in total. *Health Services Journal.*

Center for Diseases Control. (2020). *Severe Outcomes Among Patients with Coronavirus Disease 2019 (Covid-19).* Retrieved from Center for Diseases Control: https://www.cdc.gov/mmwr/volumes/69/wr/mm6912e2.htm

Dichter, J. K. (2014). System-level planning, coordination, and communication: care of the critically ill and injured during pandemics and disasters: CHEST consensus statement. *Chest,* 146(4 Suppl).

GPICS. (2019). Guidelines for the Provision of Intensive Care Services (GPICS). Faculty of Intensive Care Medicine and The Intensive Care Society.

Intensive Care Society. (2021). *Recovery and Restitution of Critical Care.*

Kaplan, L. J. (2020). Critical Care Clinician Reports on Coronavirus Disease 2019 Results From a National Survey of 4,875 ICU Providers. *Critical Care Explorations:.*

Low, D. (2004). SARS: lessons from Toronto. In M. A. Knobler S, *Institute of Medicine (US) Forum on Microbial Threats.* Washington (DC): National Academies Press (US).

Macdonald, B. a. (2018). *Systems Leadership: Creating Positive Organisations.* Routledge.

Rhodes, A. F. (2012). The variability of critical care bed numbers in Europe. *Intensive Care Medicine*, 1647-1653.

Summers, C. (2021, March). *Any Covid inquiry must help us 'fix the roof' before the next pandemic hits.* Retrieved from https://www.theguardian.com/commentisfree/2021/mar/18/covid-inquiry-pandemic-britain-woeful-unpreparedness

Wang, D. H. (2020). Clinical characteristics of 138 hospitalized patients with 2019 novel coronavirus-infected pneumonia in Wuhan, China. *JAMA*.

World Health Organisation. (2020, March). Retrieved from https://www.who.int/news-room/detail/03-03-2020-shortage-of-personal-protective-equipment-endangering-health-workers-worldwide

7

How the Australian court system adapted

WRITTEN BY DON FARRANDS QC

14 August 2021

The courts must necessarily make adjustments to the administration of justice in an attempt to deal with the covid19 pandemic. But what should guide the changes?

ABSTRACT: In response to the Covid-19 pandemic, the Courts could simply move to 'online' and other non-physical Court processes– but such expediency should only be taken after careful prior analysis of how such changes may affect the experience of participants in the legal process and the perception of the public based on fundamental values such as fairness, trust, honesty and respect for human dignity.

Introduction

Quite a lot has already been written about the impact of the Covid-19 pandemic and the Court systems, both here in Australia and abroad.[1]

In the main, Courts have sought to deal with the pandemic by side-stepping the 'in person' elements of the administration of justice as much as possible, principally by avoiding physical buildings and spaces, and by introducing technology, in particular video-link hearings. And, as has been observed, brought-in at break-neck speed.[2] Additionally, some fundamental pillars of justice, such as the jury system, have been suspended or undergone major changes.

Despite the flexibility of the Courts to seek to deal with the pandemic by such means, it has been said that there remains a "gaping hole of understanding of the overall impact of online hearings on the quality of justice."[3]

As will be sought to be illustrated later in this paper, if careful analysis of the kind described below is not undertaken before changes are made to seek to address the Covid-19 risks, such changes may (although not always) have significant unintended and adverse consequences on the administration of justice. The analysis should be region or country specific because a particular change may work well in one region/country but not in another; a proposed change must be analysed by reference, inter alia, to how the change is likely to be viewed by litigants in that region/country, and the public generally.

This paper suggests that before changes are made so as to protect against Covid-19, it is desirable to seek to predict how those changes by Court leaders will be judged, positively or negatively, by participants in the legal process and the public against what are arguably universal and unchanging values common to all cultures, namely honesty, fairness, trust, respect for human dignity, and love. In the context of court systems based on the common law tradition and in the Australian experience in particular, the thesis of the paper is that if this work is not done, it is possible that although litigants and the public may well be better protected from the risks of Covid-19, the standing of the Courts might nevertheless be diminished and therefore their effectiveness in achieving the purpose of the Courts also diminished rather than enhanced.

When deciding whether changes are appropriate in the context of the Covid-19 pandemic, those with the authority to make changes should therefore take into account how litigants and the public in the relevant culture, are likely to view the changes.

To illustrate the above, several possible changes are discussed below. Three in particular dealt with below are: changes to the jury system; changes involving online Court hearings; changes to the 'openness' of the Courts.

Before turning to those illustrations, it is important to lay the groundwork for the analysis, namely to outline both the fundamental purpose of the Courts and various means by which they seek to achieve their purpose over time.

Fundamental purpose of the Courts

In general terms, all Courts in democratic societies have the same overriding purpose: to aid the cohesion of society by giving reasonable access to justice, quelling disputes peacefully (rather than through violence), enforcing rights and obligations (with consistency), dealing with misconduct (including crimes), and regulating/reviewing Government decisions. The Covid pandemic is another challenge to which the institution must respond and adapt in line with the culture in which courts work.[4]

To illustrate in more detail the nature of this challenge, consider the example of the Supreme Court of Victoria. Its goal and purpose is stated as:[5]

Goal: To be a modern superior court that is accessible to and trusted by all, fulfilling a fundamental role in our democratic society.

Purpose: To serve the community by upholding the law through just, independent and impartial decision making and dispute resolution.

Systems, symbols and behaviours within Courts

The longevity of the courts such as the Supreme Court of Victoria in Australia and in other common law countries, owes much to the way in which the courts have maintained their reputations by delivering justice impartially, fearlessly, and cost effectively. In doing so, they have sought to reflect changing cultural norms (normative standards) and values and have sought to enforce those norms and values with consistency.

At the individual level, a Court might be said to be achieving its purpose if litigants and the public are able to say 'I trust the Court', or 'it has treated me fairly', or are able to make similar such expressions, as demonstrate that the litigant's view of the Court is viewed positively against the core values, namely honesty, fairness, trust, respect for human dignity, and love. When so doing, a litigant or a member of the public will necessarily be assessing the systems, symbols and behaviours of and within the Courts.

Just as systems, symbols and behaviours within Courts will be judged according to such values, so too will changes to systems, symbols and behaviours by the Courts in response to CV-19. These will be judged against shared assumptions and beliefs as to what is viewed positively (or negatively) against the fundamental values referred to earlier. Some values will be in play more than others (i.e. some may be neutral on the spectrum (continuum) of values, that is, between extremely negative and positive values). In this context, the above values are likely to be to the fore in how those participating in and who are directly impacted by the justice system views the Court's changes to its pre-pandemic processes.

If society rates the Covid-19 related changes positively against these values, the experience can strengthen social cohesion and the reputation of the Courts, but the contrary may also apply.[6]

Whether particular systems, symbols and behaviours in the Courts are in fact seen by litigants and the public as positive is a separate question from the leadership's intent - the Court's changes may in fact be viewed negatively - with people saying for example 'the system is 'unfair because although the risk of Covid is much lower, I didn't get my say', or 'the result was unjust because as far as I could tell over the video-link the judge was against me' or 'I didn't trust the process because it was confusing and seemed too distant'.

As will be illustrated below, it is the plenary work of those who have the authority to change the way the Courts work, namely the leadership of the Courts, to assess how such changes are likely to be viewed, and importantly, to do that assessment *before* changes are made. This then gives the opportunity to revise if necessary, the suggested changes so as to integrate the reason for the change, namely Covid-19 safety, into the object of maintaining the standing and purpose of the Court.

First example: should juries be suspended? If not, what are the implications of 'work around' arrangements under which juries are retained in a Covid-19 safe way (if possible)?

It is a precept of the justice system that for major criminal cases, issues of fact should be determined by a jury of the accused's peers.[7] It has been observed that citizen participation in the legal system is considered to be central to a healthy democracy,[8] and research shows that juries are effective in promoting the authority of the Courts.[9]

In pandemics, however, it is open for the leadership within the Court (or the executive arm of government), to consider suspending the jury system in order to keep the public (the jurors) safe, or to change the work arrangements of juries to accommodate the Covid-19 risk.

Suspending jury trials is a real problem for the criminal justice system; accused on remand are left there; accused on bail have their lives put on hold; trials get back-logged putting more pressure on the Courts in the future.

There are further significant implications of suspending the jury system during the Covid-19 pandemic. It is likely that with Covid-19, there is already very significant government intervention in society's normal dealings. It is possible that, although suspending juries may be the safest option for jurors (and Court staff), nevertheless, this may be viewed by the public as an unnecessary erosion of a fundamental protection afforded to citizens against state control; that factual findings in a criminal trial are to be determined by peers, not by judges (a form of societal control on the determination of 'the truth'). This may well be particularly so in America where the notion of judgment by peers is a particularly keen concept of justice. The change may result in the public (or some members of it) viewing the criminal justice system as less trustworthy.

It follows that the Court should consider any such fundamental system change very carefully.

But even if the Court or the executive arm of government seeks to retain the jury system during the Covid-19 pandemic, the leadership will need to assess carefully how changes to accommodate Covid-19 risk are likely to be viewed.

For example, although some parts of the jury process may be able to be put online, such as empanelling the jury, other parts may still need to be in person. This may suggest the need for the establishment of two or more jury rooms. But even this may be viewed with suspicion or mistrust by some jurors if they are split between rooms.

A further option is to have more physical Court rooms, where there is less 'foot traffic'. In the UK, jury trials have been run in cinemas and other entertainment complexes. This obviously raises the question of a change in symbols and systems, no doubt affecting the defendant's and each juror's perception of whether the defendant, now being tried in a cinema for example, is being treated fairly.

However, criminal matters which do not involve a jury, such as a plea hearing, can and have been done via video link. A good example is the plea of guilty given by Brenton Tarrant in New Zealand on 26 March 2020, which was taken via video link. The prisoner was taken to be "present".[10]

If juries are to be retained, one option might be to make it compulsory for jurors to be vaccinated. The system owner (the legislature) should do the analysis of considering the likely consequences of making it a pre-condition of a juror's selection that they be vaccinated against Covid-19 (in effect, making vaccinations compulsory). It may on careful analysis be concluded that compulsory vaccinations are viewed positively in some countries (potentially Australia) but negatively in others, such as in America, where such compulsion may be viewed as a severe invasion of civil liberties, and therefore an inroad into the individual dignity of a citizen. In America, this might even produce the result that the Court system is viewed as untrustworthy because it is an inflexible organ of the state.

These issues highlight the complexity of any system change, particularly one involving fundamental rights and responsibilities.

Second example: should the Court move to online hearings (in whole or in part)?

The Court Building and its Significance

Since Roman times, it has been a principle of virtually all justice systems in the western world that the law of a jurisdiction, whether criminal or civil, is enforced 'by and in Court'.

An obvious and significant symbol of the justice system is the Court house itself. The Court as a 'place' has real significance for the rule of law.[11] In virtually all communities, the Court house is an imposing and prominent building. When citizens enter it, it is re-enforced to them that the legal system, in particular the judiciary, has the authority of the State to impose the rule of law.

In cities, for example, often the Court house or Court building, is a significant historical structure, with a grand entrance, high ceilings, and long corridors. In country regions, it may be that the Court house is the most significant building for miles around. There is usually a security system through which dangerous objects or persons are filtered. Court staff are dressed in formal uniforms. The Court conducts its business at its discretion – you cannot say 'I would like to start my case at 11am instead of 10am.' Except for urgent proceedings, cases come on according to the management of the Court's business.

In short, the Court's authority is enhanced by the physical Court building and its processes within it. In general terms, the higher the Court, the more significant the building.

As we will see, a move away from the use of such buildings is likely to have significant implications for the administration of justice.

The Courtroom and its Significance

Equally, within the Courthouse, the physical aspects of a courtroom itself should be noted. The Judge usually sits high above the other participants, as part spectator, part umpire. Counsel stand behind 'the bar' table, in equal measure (a system of equalisation[12]), some distance from the Judge.

In criminal cases, the accused stands in 'the dock'. In non-criminal (civil) trials there is no such dock. This is one way (of many[13]) criminal trials are differentiated from civil trials. The differentiation, based on the different nature of the work, is highly symbolic. Streamlining court procedures by using video links moves participants away from the physical court room and may well be expedient from a Covid-19 perspective.

However, care must be taken to ensure a system which is one of differentiation is not changed in the process to one of equalisation without clear justification. Providing a Covid-19 safe court environment for all is a system of equalisation. It is possible however, that by retaining some of the symbols associated with the trial of people accused of crimes, people may regard the Courts as being less caring (loving) of the need for the Courts to facilitate the safety of the public.

These physical dimensions to the administration of justice are fundamental and long lasting. The durability and standing of the Courts in the community is supported by these symbols which align with the values of fairness and trust, and respect for the dignity. Costumes in Court (black gowns, wigs and the like) are also intended to aide in building fairness and trust, because, inter alia, the persuasion of the advocates is to primarily be determined by what they say and do rather than who they are.

The significance of physical appearances has been well studied and recognised. For example,[14] in 2009 in the UK, video link appearances were unsuccessfully introduced into Magistrate Court hearings, the change being seen as an 'isolating process'. And in 2017, the group Transform Justice reviewed the impact of video link hearings in the UK and concluded that "virtual technology inevitably degrades the quality of human interaction", and that "nuances may be undetected, [with] misunderstandings may go un-noticed more easily".

When a pandemic breaks out

In a pandemic, for the safety of citizens, the Court building is shut, or given heavily restricted operating hours. Therefore courtrooms cease to be used or are also heavily restricted in their use. In New Zealand, for example, on 26 March 2020, in an unprecedented move, the District and High Courts were closed to members of the public whose presence was not required for the conduct of business.

The closing of the courts is in itself a statement of the values of the administration of justice, namely that during a pandemic people should be physically safe in the course of seeking and obtaining justice. As the annual report of the Victorian Supreme Court indicates, by June 2020, in that court hundreds of hearings went online, and most of the court's judicial officers and staff were operating off-site.[15]

When the pandemic struck, the Supreme Court of Victoria for example activated its Business Continuity Plan, supported by a team drawn from across different areas of the Court. As part of that response, a Virtual Hearing Taskforce was established on 19 March 2020 to oversee the development of broader solutions, processes and procedures to support a virtual hearing model, where matters could be heard with some or all participants connecting remotely.[16]

When Courthouses and courtrooms are shut or become inaccessible, a significant set of Court systems and symbols of authority become absent, or at least less apparent/observable. The Supreme Court of Victoria considered that a plan was required which would enable the Courts to continue to function by explaining the basis of the changes made, identifying potential negative reactions and how these would be a handled by the Court and its non-judicial officers.

There are a number of ways a Court might seek to deal with the public's Covid-19 risk in a way which minimises changes to courthouse access and courtroom use. Courts could do, and have done, a number of things to maintain at least some physical access to a Court building and processes within it. Courts have for example:

- permitted access for 'pandemic safe' hearings, involving a single person or persons in the Court;
- ensured as appropriate that at least Judges and staff (or some of them) continue to operate from the Court building (or are seen in video conferencing with litigants to be present at the building);
- given regular updates to the public as to when the Court will or is likely to re-open.

In assessing whether these processes should be put in place, the leadership of the Courts should seek to determine how such processes are likely to be viewed by litigants and the public. For example, if the courtroom is open to some but not all litigants, this may be viewed as 'unfair', particularly where the reasoning for the difference is not made clear. Similarly, if some Courts are open but not others, and yet the pandemic is pervasive, this may adversely affect how people perceive the Courts; again, where a system of equalisation is changed to a system of differentiation, for no apparent reason.

As the Law Council of Australia has recently indicated,[17] face-to-face relationships between lawyers and marginalised and vulnerable communities are often crucial to building trust and respect, both of which are important in securing positive justice outcomes.

'Social processes' within a Courtroom

The work of the Court is one of deciding which of the possible outcomes put to it by the parties is the most 'just' having regard to the rule of law. This is often a very difficult question, involving fine points of detail, assessment, and analysis.

It is in part the social processes[18] established within a Court hearing which are intended to facilitate the reasoning process, and in turn the outcome decided by the Court.

Such 'social processes' include the following procedures, protocols and behaviours.

As to the authority of the Court:

- the insistence of courtesy at all times to all parties and all witnesses, as regulated by the presiding Judge;
- deference to the authority of the Judge, and conferring dignity on the Judge and other participants in the process, by referring to them as 'Your Honour' and 'my learned friend', emphasising the plenary value of the Court, fairness and honesty through honourable conduct and judgment.

As to the reasoning process:

- the insistence that only one person speak at a time (a process which also respects human dignity);
- the insistence that there be a formal step-by-step process of submissions by each party, with reply submissions – the reasoning process is essentially didactic in nature;
- the overall techniques of persuasion are deployed to arrive at a 'just' conclusion.

The question arises within the Covid-19 pandemic as to whether the social processes within a physical court process can be dealt with by non-physical court processes, namely in video-link type court hearings.

It is not clear whether the above particular 'social processes' are able to be observed equally via video-link court hearings. There must be some risk that because of the 'remoteness' of video hearings, counsel and the Judge may not fully engage on complex issues where the pathway to resolution requires extensive discussion with counsel.

It is also arguable that a video link inhibits 'didactic' processes and encourages a shorter timeframe in which to seek to determine the issues in question.

It is also arguable that video-link court work may inhibit counsel's ability to persuade the Court to a particular result.

The 'cost' of using video-links has been described as follows:[19]

Not only are rewards lessened via these social disconnections during videoconferencing, but there are also elevated costs in the form of cognitive effort. Much of communication is actually unconscious and non-verbal, as emotional content is rapidly processed through social cues like touch, joint attention, and body posture.[16] These nonverbal cues are not only used to acquire information about others, but are also directly used to prepare an adaptive response and engage in reciprocal communication, all in a matter of milliseconds.[17] However, on video, most of these cues are difficult to visualize, since the same environment is not shared (limiting joint attention) and both subtle facial expressions and full bodily gestures may not be captured. Without the help of these unconscious cues on which we have relied since infancy to socioemotionally assess each other and bond, compensatory cognitive and emotional effort is required.

The Courts should determine whether any additional steps should be introduced into the Court's 'reasoning processes' to deal with such potential pitfalls outlined above as to online hearings. It may be that counsel should be consulted in that regard so that an assessment can be made as to whether counsel consider that the reasoning processes have been diminished. If they have been, this may indicate that the 'fairness' of the process will be diminished unless such additional steps are introduced.

Assessing the demeanour of a witness: in-person versus online

It is well established that a Judge, if a trier of fact, is entitled, indeed, under a duty, to assess the veracity of the evidence of a witness by reference to the whole of the evidence given, and may take into account the demeanour (behaviour) of the witness. The same considerations apply where a jury is assessing witness evidence in determining the facts of a particular case.

The High Court of Australia has stated in regard to the giving of oral evidence that:[20

"The adducing of oral evidence from witnesses in criminal trials underlies the rules of procedure which the law ordains for their conduct. A witness who gives evidence orally demonstrates, for good or ill, more about his or credibility than a witness whose evidence is given in documentary form..... Oral evidence gives the trial the atmosphere which, though intangible, is often critical to the jury's estimate of the witness."

Further, observations have been made by various Courts about the un-desirability of the accused appearing behind glass or Perspex screens, as if they were appearing by video link.[21]

Further, there is research which suggests victims and witnesses testifying live are perceived to be more honest and convincing when compared to those on video link.[22] This is said to be partly because physical appearance is more vivid and therefore memorable.[23]

These are all important if not vital considerations relating to a possible move to online hearings. A litigant might well contend, on a finding by the Court that the demeanour of the witness/litigant went against them; that the online process exaggerated the impugned conduct.

This is yet another example of the need by the Court to assess a change to online cases by reference to how the change is likely to be viewed by litigants and the public.

Other aspects of online hearings

Of course online hearings are safer against the risk of infection from the Covid-19 virus than physical hearings.

In addition to the complex issues discussed earlier, there are other important aspects which should be taken into account when deciding whether to move to an online system of hearings, some of which are touched on as follows.

First, some litigants may view the online system as less 'personal', that is, that the 'system' has gone from being dealt with by a real person, to more of a computer-based decision-making process. The litigant may feel that there is less human dignity being afforded to the litigant via online processes than Courtroom processes in person. This may or may not in fact be so but it is the likely perception of the litigant which must be assessed before any change is made.

Second, litigants may consider that although they have access to participate online, there is less opportunity to 'have one's say' in the online environment.

Third, there may be less opportunity, without formal processes being put in place, for a client to confer with their legal presentative in private or even during the hearing.

Fourth, some litigants may not have access to computer systems and therefore may wish to seek a hearing in person, even if the Covid-19 risk exists.

Fifth, although costs are likely to be lower for online hearings, for some litigants, cost alone may not be viewed as a significant issue and therefore a hearing in person may be preferred.

Sixth, in some countries the risk of contracting Covid-19 is very low (such as in Australia) whereas in other countries, the risk is very high (such as Brazil). It may be that online hearings are seen as unfair in some countries compared to the risk of infection whereas in other countries, the change is seen as entirely justifiable.

Seventh, while giving the appearance of efficiency, an online hearing may inhibit constructive dialogue between opposing parties who may have reached agreement or consent on important matters had there been a physical hearing.

These aspects may give rise to a sense that an online platform is either 'unfair' or 'fair' or even 'untrustworthy' ('why move to an online system when the risk is so low') or 'trustworthy' (the 'change was necessary to protect us').

Thus, while going to an online hearing system may seem obvious at first blush, nevertheless there are complex fairness, trust and human dignity issues associated with doing so.

Studies on the impact of a move to online hearings

Whether the Court is able to persuade citizens that a 'virtual court' provides a satisfactory alternative to a physical Court is an open question and no doubt will be the subject of study and academic writing for some time. As has been observed "introducing monitors into the courtroom requires a reimagining of courtroom spaces, social cues, symbols and performances".[24]

In at least one study, it has been found that criminal defendants on a screen are no more likely to be found guilty than defendants sitting next to a legal representative.[25] However, there do appear to be biases or inequalities. It has been observed[26] that there is data showing that:

- defendants 'in the dock' are more likely to be found guilty;
- defendants in the US who appear online in jail are more likely to have higher bail and sentences imposed than those defendants that sit behind their legal representative in the courtroom;
- asylum-seekers in the US appearing remotely online are more likely to be deported than those that attend the courtroom.

Mitigation steps

It has been suggested that if a party feels isolated from the Court's processes, it is more likely that they will not perceive the process as "fair".[27] Attempts have been made to limit this sense of 'remoteness' by having individual screens for individual participants (Judge, legal representative, litigant/defendant).[28] However, as observed earlier, there are serious adverse issues associated with video link hearings and these kinds of initiatives may have only limited off-setting effect.

What is important is that even without a building and courtroom, the authority of the Court is maintained, and that plans are in place to manage an absence of a physical Court to address any perceived unfairness and avoid any perceived unfair processes or lack of trust issues arising.

It is for the leadership within the Court to determine how best to do this but it should do so by reference to how such a system and symbol change is likely to be viewed.

Third example: should the courtroom even if open to litigants, be closed to the public?

It is also a plenary precept of justice that Courts be open to the public, unless there are good public policy reasons for their work being conducted 'in camera' (in closed session).[29] By being open, the public can see for itself the Court at work, assess the quality of the work of the judicial officer, and of other officers of the Court including counsel. It is by being able to visit and sit in Courts that the public can view and review the judicial system in operation.

This not only applies to the 'lay public' but to people who may be connected to a particular Court case; they can go along, hear the Judge, hear what counsel and witnesses say, and make their own judgements about the fairness and trustworthiness of what is going on.

But in a pandemic, the Court may decide that although litigants should be able to be physically present, the public should not.

Although the Courts have a number of technological tools enabling a limited amount of 'openness', not every case in every Court can be 'streamed'. It follows that some cases will be 'closed'.

The Court must nevertheless, in seeking to apply the principle of 'openness', decide which cases should be made generally available to the public. One such case is the recent decision of the Supreme Court of Victoria to publicly stream an inquiry into the fees charged by counsel in a class action, in which it has been alleged that the fees were excessive and/or obtained improperly.

As with the earlier illustrations, a decision by a Court to 'close its doors' to the public is a significant one and should be the subject of analysis as to how such a decision will be viewed by the public. If only some cases are 'streamed', this may suggest to some members of the public that there is not complete transparency of the judicial process, which may erode trust, even though the very selection of certain cases is intended to *enhance* trust.

Conclusion

It is certainly the case that the pandemic has required significant changes to the way justice is administered by one of the three organs of Government, the judiciary.

Great care must be taken to ensure that the established precepts are preserved to the extent practicable. This can only be sought to be done by understanding the implications of the changes in systems, symbols and behaviours within the Courts, assessed by determining how litigants and the public are likely to view the changes against the universal values referred to earlier, including fairness, trust and honesty.

How Courts should seek, other than by their own assessments, to predict the likely beliefs of litigants and the public is a topic unto its own for a separate occasion.

Apart from seeking to assess the beliefs, there is also the question of the specific controls which should be put in place to monitor the experience and perceptions of members of the Court, litigants and the public over time. The outcomes of such monitoring should be the subject of further study and policy consideration. That too is a topic unto itself.

* * *

Notes

[1] I reference some of the literature later in this paper.

[2] *How Remote? - videolinks and justice in the Victorian Courts*, Tom Battersby, Issue 169 Winter 2021 Victorian Bar News, p40 at 41.

[3] *What will courtroom justice look like in the future?* Jacqui Horan, Victorian Bar News, Issue 168 Summer 2020/21, 39.

[4] See *Systems Leadership- creating positive organisations.* Macdonald I , Burke C and Stewart K. 2nd Edition Routledge, 2018 p 327.

[5] Supreme Court of Victoria, Annual Report.

[6] see *Systems Leadership – Creating Positive Organisations*, ibid, pp 64 - 67.

[7] See for example *R v Pell*. Pell was ultimately acquitted by the High Court of Australia, having been convicted by a jury trial. See *Pell v The Queen* [2020] 94 ALJR 394. Although the jury determines the facts, the jury is told by the Judge what the law is. It is sometimes determined that a Judge should try both issues of fact and law as a sole decision maker.

[8] *What will courtroom justice look like in the future?* (ibid), 41.

[9] See J Delahunty, N Brewer, J Clough, J Horan, J Ogloff, D Tait, J Pratley et al, Practices, Policies and Procedures that influence Juror Sat-

isfaction in Australia (2008) Australian Institute of Criminology; J Horan, *Perceptions of the Civil Jury System* (2005) 31 MULR 120.

[10] For a more detailed description of the plea, see Journal of Civil Litigation and Practice, Vol 9/1 of 2020, *Courts and Covid-19: Delivering the Rule of Law in a Time of Crisis,* David Harvey, 59, at 63.

[11] For a detailed explanation of this, see Dame Helen Winkelmann, "A framework for the Future: Technology and the Rule of Law" (Paper presented at the Australasian Supreme and Federal Court Judges' Conference, Canberra, 20 January 2020).

[12] In other words, a system where the participants in the system are treated equally as opposed to differentially.

[13] An obvious other difference is the differing onus of proof (in criminal trials, the onus is 'beyond reasonable doubt', in civil trials it is ' on the balance of probabilities').

[14] See *How Remote? – videolinks and justice in the Victorian Courts,* Tom Battersby, Issue 169 Winter 2021 Victorian Bar News, p40 at 41.

[15] Annual report 2019-20, Supreme Court of Victoria, Joint Foreword, p11.

[16] Annual report 2019-20, Supreme Court of Victoria, Court Snapshot, p14.

[17] As cited in *How Remote? – videolinks and justice in the Victorian Courts,* Tom Battersby, Issue 169 Winter 2021 Victorian Bar News, p40 at 41.

[18] The ability to interact with others at work to produce a productive outcome: As outlined in *Systems Leadership – Creating Positive Organisations,* 2nd Ed, Ian Macdonald, Catherine Burke, Karl Stewart, Rout-

ledge, 2018, , 32. Among other things, social process is required for handling confrontations: *Systems Leadership* (ibid), 89.

[19] A Neuropsychological Exploration of Zoom Fatigue, November 18, 2020, Jena Lee, MD.

[20] *Butera v Director of Public Prosecutions (Vic)* [1987] HCA 58, [15].

[21] See the examples cited in *How Remote? – videolinks and justice in the Victorian Courts*, Tom Battersby, Issue 169 Winter 2021 Victorian Bar News, p40 at 42.

[22] See Sara Landstrom, Karl Ask & Charlotte Sommar, *Credibility judgments in context: effects of emotional expression, presentation mode, and statement consistency*, (2019) 25(3), *Psychology, Crime and Law.*

[23] *How Remote? – videolinks and justice in the Victorian Courts*, Tom Battersby, Issue 169 Winter 2021 Victorian Bar News, p40 at 42 and the study reference there.

[24] D Tait and M Rossner 'Courts are moving to video during coronavirus, but research shows it's hard to get a fair trial remotely'. *The Conversation* (8 April 2020), cited in *What will courtroom justice look like in the future?* (ibid), 39.

[25] D Tait, B McKimmie, R Sarre, D Jones, L McDonald and K Gelb, *Towards a Distributed Courtroom* (2017).

[26] See *What will courtroom justice look like in the future?* (ibid), 39, and the references therein.

[27] *What will courtroom justice look like in the future?* (ibid), 39-40.

[28] *What will courtroom justice look like in the future?* (ibid), 40.

[29] For example, perhaps in a terrorist trial.

8

Newmont mining – Employee Engagement and Community Partnership

WRITTEN BY TOM PALMER

Introduction: Leading Through Change

The first week of March 2020 was a busy time at Newmont. Our annual Global Leadership Meeting was planned for the following week in Southern California, and details were being finalized for the agenda and working sessions. From speakers to seating, the event was designed to foster engagement among our top 100 leaders, introduce new team members and energize the group following a transformational 2019 that involved the acquisition of Goldcorp and the establishment of a major joint venture in Nevada. The meeting was traditionally held off-site, away from Newmont's corporate office, and leaders traveled from around the world to participate in this much anticipated annual session. However, world events were unfolding fast.

The World Health Organization had just officially declared a global pandemic of a virus called Covid-19 and my executive leadership and I were on high-alert. *If the threat related to the virus continued to escalate, would our team members be able to travel back to their homes after the meeting? What if someone fell ill and exposed other leaders, all in close proximity for several days?* There were many unknowns. Though the meeting had taken months of planning, the potential risks to our people and business in any scenario were simply not worth the risk. By midweek, we had decided: We would not expose Newmont's leaders to a potential health risk and instead pivot from an in–person to a virtual Global Leadership Meeting. Within days, the meeting schedule had been condensed to accommodate a virtual format, and our Information Technology team had meeting rooms across our regional and corporate offices synched for the session.

On March 10th, we commenced our first fully virtual Global Leadership Meeting. On the second day, several leaders were missing from the sessions. They had been informed of a positive exposure to the virus at a conference the previous week and requested to isolate from others. These individuals immediately went into quarantine at home, but with the new meeting format, were able to participate in the session without any impact. In one day, it was clear: Our decision to prioritize safety and quickly transition to a virtual format not only kept our team members safe, but allowed inclusive engagement that would not have been possible in a traditional face-to-face meeting format.

By Friday, March 13, the Global Leadership Meeting had wrapped up, however, it was evident that the threat from Covid-19 had not. We advised team members in our Denver corporate office, and at all of our locations around the globe, to take what equipment and supplies they needed to facilitate remote work. Little did these people know, for most of them, it would be more than a year before they returned to an office environment—and for some, when they returned, it would even be to a different building.

Looking Back: A Year of Change

A year later, we were planning another Global Leadership Meeting. It was again in a virtual format but this time for two reasons: first, the world was still battling with the global pandemic and second, the experiences of the previous year had proven that remote working could deliver both collaboration and performance. While Newmont, like the rest of the world, was impacted by the coronavirus, our response to the pandemic, driven by our organization's values, and anchored in the tenants of systems leadership, positioned us to weather the storm and emerge stronger. In the third quarter of 2020, Newmont saw its best-ever safety performance and strongest quarter in its 100-year history. The year-end results sent investors and shareholders a resounding message: We were not only holding our place as the industry leader, but growing stronger despite the pandemic headwinds. A boost in gold price added to our strong performance; yet, I believe that utilizing a pragmatic leadership approach, leveraging a clear decision-making framework and creating an environment that allowed our team members to rally together to find opportunity in challenge cemented our position of strength.

Newmont is the world's largest gold company, operating on four continents and in nine different countries. With approximately 26,000 employees and contractors, it would be impossible to highlight all the incredible stories of the people and teams who worked together to support each other and safely generate sustainable results throughout the worst pandemic in a hundred years. This paper will highlight the framework that helped clarify the work of my leadership team and our approach to the virus response, key challenges, decision points, lessons learned and the long-term impact on both our workforce and how we partner with local communities. As I put pen to paper, the pandemic rages on; vaccines have reached many of our US and Canadian based personnel, but it is anticipated to be some time before the vaccine is accessible to many around the world. I must also acknowledge that we have lost team members to the virus. As I reflect not only on our response to Covid-19, but on the leaders and teams who have remained committed to our business despite challenging circumstances and heartbreak, I acknowledge, that in many ways, Newmont will never be the same.

Covid-19 Response: Fundamentals and Framework

Our response to this pandemic required agility, trust and flexibility across my extended leadership team. This situation was fundamentally different than any of us—or the world---had faced before; we did not have the traditional luxury of meeting together, where we can use all of our senses to understand social process and help guide a response. Instead, we navigated new technologies and the fatigue associated with multiple time zones to respond to a crisis with more questions than answers and where circumstances changed by the hour. Our cohesive response required a framework to provide a path through the unknown, a framework that mapped the work of a leader and helped cut through complexity; this structure ensured that contributions could be made and clear decisions taken.

My first priority was to set the context, which global headlines and media updates helped do by the minute. The pandemic was a mammoth challenge that required all leaders to be united in the "why" of their response. We developed a purpose statement to help guide our work in this complex environment: *To work together, in accordance with our values, to protect our people and business through this unprecedented crisis.*

With clear context and purpose, a framework for our response came together: We would need to identify critical issues, seek contributions from the across the business and make clear decisions to move forward. Tasks would be assigned with clear accountabilities; details and data would need to be monitored. Gathering feedback was critical so we could adjust and refine decisions as needed, learning together, as the world and business evolved.

A very important component of our framework was a set of guiding principles which were developed to support our decision making. These were:

- We will put the safety and well-being of our workforce and local communities at the forefront of every decision and err on the side of caution when determining risk tolerance in decision making.
- We will demonstrate through our behavior to our employees that they are our most valued resource in our response to this worldwide crisis.
- We will make decisions that consider long-term impacts, not just short-term answers.
- We will make decisions that encourage the right behaviors and outcomes.
- We will communicate frequently and transparently.

In addition to these steps, working with my team I developed a strategic scenario planning framework to evaluate the potential impacts on our workforce, local communities and our business across multiple phases, or waves of the virus. These three waves addressed the current situation and predicted future impacts on our operations based on available data and worldwide trends. The analysis included timelines, considerations and potential impact in areas including: case trends by countries and jurisdictions where we operate; benchmark countries, and what is changing/has changed.

With each wave, we worked diligently to develop both business continuity plans and a people-specific response. Business continuity plans were established at the site level to ensure safe operations and/or care and maintenance for our operations and helped mitigate economic impact; they also incorporated region-specific considerations and talent needs. The People approach ensured support for our workforce. This included alignment on concerns, scenarios, issues and addressed key topics such as Total Rewards, Talent Management and Employee Wellbeing.

A robust communications plan was also developed with transparent messages sent on a regular cadence. These messages reinforced our organization's values—safety, integrity, sustainability, inclusion, responsibility—and centered around three key themes:

- Newmont will place the health, safety and wellbeing of our people and communities above all else
- We are in this together with our local communities and host governments
- The strength of Newmont's business, leadership and operating model underpins our ability to effectively manage this crisis

While my team had jurisdictional limitations and legal requirements to consider, the decision-making framework, strategic "waves" approach, monitoring of data and metrics and a pragmatic willingness to learn and evolve helped chart our path through months of uncertainty.

Wave I – March – June 2020

The first "wave" of the pandemic found me and my Leadership Team in a full-court press to quickly respond, to stabilize and settle the workforce. During early mornings and late nights on virtual meetings via WebEx we outlined a center-led response to support our workforce through the peak of the pandemic. Employees were fearful—of getting sick, of losing their jobs and of the unknown. This global approach provided initial continuity to alleviate fears and steady our employee base.

Employee Support

Employee support through this time was focused on the holistic wellbeing of our workforce—physical, mental and financial—and we took action, demonstrating love and respect, in tangible ways. First, we provided several months of financial certainty with pay continuation from the start of the pandemic through to August 2020 for all employees who could not work. Regional and corporate teams shifted to a remote work format. The global IT team helped get necessary equipment to employees at home. The HR team updated leave programs to reflect the realities of Covid-19 and communicated Employee Assistance Programs to support mental and financial resilience. The communications team set up a global email for questions, an intranet site to house "FAQs" and leaders proactively checked in with their team members; anonymous surveys were also distributed to monitor employee wellbeing. I also sent regular global updates, working to equip my leaders with talking points so there was alignment in response to questions across the globe. The result: Employees not only felt supported, but when it mattered most, saw our purpose in action. "We have a tremendously dedicated and committed workforce at Newmont," noted Jen Cmil, my Executive Vice President, Human Resources. "Our response with pay, benefits and leadership support needed to not only match the dedication of our employees, but send a clear message: Our people are our most valued asset."

Community Support

Consistent with our organization's purpose *to create value and improve lives through sustainable and responsible mining,* the natural next step was to take action to directly support host communities where we operate, providing assistance with community health efforts, food security and local economic resiliency. On April 9th, we established the Newmont Global Community Support Fund, $20 million dollars committed to assist local, regional and national level efforts in the jurisdictions that host our businesses. A formal process was established for fund allocation ensuring that assistance targeted where help was needed most. Examples of initial assistance include support of the only two (at the time) Covid-19 testing centers in Ghana and provision of protective and medical equipment to hospitals, schools and local communities. Through this fund, we have been able to act as a catalyst for long-term resiliency and support future community development.

Operations

Our operations felt the full force of Covid-19, but teamwork, resilience and an agile response to changing conditions assisted in the protection of our people and business. The health and safety of Newmont's workforce was foundational and yet, the decision to place some operations in care and maintenance, with the backdrop of an uncertain timeframe and unknown investor response, was daunting. In Wave I, we placed five of our 12 managed operations into care and maintenance; with proactively making the decision on two of them to ensure we prevented any spread of the virus to vulnerable First Nation communities living nearby. The timeframe for closure was unknown, yet our leaders communicated honestly, frequently and courageously with all stakeholders. This behavior was a tangible example of our guiding principles in action: the safety and well-being of the workforce and local communities was at the forefront of every decision; we, as a leadership team chose to err on the side of caution when determining risk tolerance and in doing so, demonstrated love and courage.

As borders closed and commercial flights were grounded, our site and regional teams worked diligently to return people home. When our Cerro Negro operation in Argentina was placed into care and Maintenance, more than 180 expatriate employees were stranded in country. The country was in full lockdown and personal transit permits required government approval. Cross-functional teams worked tirelessly to safely get all these team members back to their families. Similarly, in Suriname, our HR team went to extensive lengths to find safe routes for 25 expatriate employees to return home to their loved ones in different countries around the world.

At sites, the "Covid-19" ways of working became the new norm, seemingly overnight. Covid-19 protocols and procedures, access control and regular testing quickly took hold. At Éléonore, our team worked with the Northern Quebec Public Health Board, the Cree Health Board and the Cree Public Safety Authorities to align on communication and actions around community protection and employee safety.

The Cree Authorities identified mining sites as a high-risk zone, resulting in a mandatory isolation of 14 days for all Cree employees returning home from work. We knew the serious impact this would have to our Cree team members and doubled efforts to increase the level of confidence of our Cree partners in regards to the effectiveness of the safety protocols we had in place. By sharing safety protocols and tailoring them according to partner's needs, the operation slowly resumed operation. Across the other side of the globe in Australia, our Tanami mine kept the operation running without interruption despite interstate border closures. Team members relocated interstate with their families, and others did not return home in between rostered swings to help keep the mine in full production. Whilst some sites remained in care and maintenance, others surpassed production expectations, illustrating that despite twelve different sites and four regions, we were truly one team and operated as such.

Across our operations, Covid-19 protocols and procedures, including remote working policies and standards, were established and teams quickly ramped up technology use. Many were surprised to find that productivity did not lag, but improved. Change that may have taken years to implement rapidly gained traction. Even in these early days, teams found the golden lining, and a small, but certain upside in the disruption.

Leadership

As teams worked together to safely deliver ounces, my Leadership Team focused on what could be next—planning for the best response and outcome to a variety of potential situations. My Executive Leadership Team met daily for the first three to four months of the crisis, delving into understand the critical issues, staying abreast of changing conditions and determining critical path activities As input to support these crucial decisions, we conducted a leader-led engagement process through all parts of the organisation. This feedback from team members across the company helped ground us in the context and challenges of Covid-19 for the typical employee and how experience varied by country and region. Our Board of Directors also shifted their working approach, leveraging technology to meet monthly; actively utilizing pre-reads, so they could effectively use meeting time to discuss the critical issues impacting the business that required their support and direction. As would be evidenced in the months to come, the work from these early months—to protect individual and organizational wellbeing, to manage through uncertainty and to learn and adjust— was fundamental to our ongoing response and ultimate success.

Wave II – July 2020- July 2021

By late July 2020, it became apparent that there would be no quick end to the pandemic. Our leaders continued to leverage our scenario planning framework to address the many decisions required to effectively manage the business through this difficult time. We launched a "Together While Apart" campaign encouraging team members to post stories and encouragements on our internal Yammer social media platform, fostering a sense of community across Newmont's many locations; sites and teams shared videos on how they were managing through Covid-19. Due to varying legal requirements, jurisdictional considerations and impact of the virus by region and country, I made the decision to move from a centralized response to a country by country approach with global oversight. The response and success stories related to Employee and Community Support, Operations, and Leadership approach continued to gain momentum. The following sections offer an insight into the response in each of these critical areas.

Employee Support

As mentioned, I took a decision early in the pandemic to maintain full pay for employees who could not work through until the end of

August 2020. However, it was clear that beyond that time frame regional and country-specific challenges required a tailored response. So, from August, we shifted to a regional and country specific pay model. Employee support and messaging was transparent and focused on helping equip and prepare our workforce for the long-term impacts of Covid-19. I gave our regional leadership teams the authority to determine fit-for-purpose solutions and a regionally determined stipend was provided in support of effective remote work for employees. Our regional offices each began to evolve their long-term working model and vision for office space. Our Australia operations, with a lower national case rate, returned employees to the regional office first, embracing a hybrid model of part remote work, part in-office collaboration. Leaders were provided coaching on how to maintain team culture, engagement and support wellbeing and productivity. As other regions, including the corporate office, wrestled with employee questions and approach, our Australian team shared lessons learned and best practices for this new way of working.

A Workforce Guideline was established to support location decisions for our employee base and a global "Fixed versus Flexible" model helped guide key decisions. Both documents, though intended to provide global guardrails, were developed as living documents with the intention to update the documents with lessons learned. Before the ink was dry, we had updates in the queue; the learnings and evolution of process and thinking have been constant.

Across the globe, our team members continued to support each other as a consequence of the environment we had been able to create through our initial Wave 1 response. In August, at our Penasquito site in Mexico, an entire kitchen crew in the dining room was quarantined due to potential virus exposure. So, the Human Resources site team stepped in, donning chef hats, and making sandwiches for the crews, keeping teams fed and production running – an example that we have seen repeated many times by our teams across the globe.

Community Support

Our community outreach continued via the Community Support Fund, enabling much needed support for communities to respond to the pandemic. One donation from Newmont contributed to the construction of an oxygen plant for the Regional Hospital in Cajamarca, Peru. In Ghana, our team organized a community radio school in partnership with local radio stations and the Ghana Education Service to assist with continuing education when local schools were forced to close to students due to the pandemic. Newmont Ghana also signed a Memorandum of Understanding with the Kumasi Center for Collaborative Research to procure equipment and setup for two infectious disease labs in host communities. At our Cripple Creek and Victor mine in Colorado, our leaders partnered with the City of Victor to provide Covid Relief Funding to nine local businesses. In Denver, at the corporate office, employees donated the funds typically earmarked for the year-end holiday party to two organizations combatting local food insecurity.

"We worked collaboratively across regions and functions and with our site teams and host communities," shared my Executive Vice President, Chief Sustainability and External Affairs Officer, Stephen Gottesfeld. "We also established a robust governance process to ensure that support was directed and delivered where it was most needed. Through the tireless efforts of our employees and the Company's Covid Community Support fund, we addressed critical health needs, food security concerns and economic resiliency challenges."

Operations

All twelve of our operating sites resumed operations by July 1 2020, with robust controls to limit potential exposure to the virus for our workforce. Sites continued to operate with reduced numbers, with some roles even working more efficiently in a remote capacity. Strict physical distancing, cleaning and screening protocols were embraced across all locations; the term "safe production" took on a whole new meaning. At sites, handwashing stations were established at strategic points, dining rooms restricted people and some established physical barriers. Teams also implemented staggered shift starts to reduce the number of employee interactions. At Penasquito in Mexico, a special isolation camp was set up for potential cases, where employees waited for results of PCR tests; in South America, where shared accommodations were the norm, Covid-19 restrictions meant a new solution was needed. Our Camps and Projects teams at Merian, Yanacocha and Cerro Negro worked diligently to develop and get approval for additional accommodations, enabling single-occupancy accommodations for site employees. At our Cripple Creek and Victor mine, the team worked with Teller County to host an on-site vaccination clinic for employees and their family members seeking inoculation for Covid-19 and the seasonal flu. Our teams worked diligently to find solutions to challenges, supporting each other and always working to keep each other safe. Leaders empowered and encouraged this creativity and met consistently to monitor issues. Our site leadership team at Porcupine, located in the city of Timmins in northeastern Ontario, held weekly WebEx Covid-19 Management meetings to stay up to date and aligned. Other site leaders did much the same.

In any situation, communication is important, yet with Covid-19, our teams sought ways to stay up to date and share information. At Cerro Negro, the team established "DoreBot," a chatbot for Whatsapp that allows employees and contractors to access important information 24 hours a day. For the initial launch, teams sent information related to bi-weekly shift changes and Covid-19, including functionality to download PCR tests, temperature control logs, and information on how to complete a Covid-19 symptoms self-assessment. With every decision and action, our leaders at Newmont using our guiding principles helped not only manage the circumstances of a crisis, but simultaneously helped build a better future for our employees and surrounding communities.

Leadership

Despite the challenges from the pandemic, in 2020, we achieved our best safety performance in company history. The commitment to health and safety of each individual was evident across the business. Through our Fatality Risk Management program, leaders conducted over 70,000 critical control interactions with team members to help understand and manage our fatality risks. By rapidly replicating and learning from each other, our teams were able to establish robust Covid-19 management plans across our business, allowing us to continue to safely operate and produce ounces that generated significant free cash flow.

The impact of care and maintenance at some operations and Covid-19 controls and restrictions did impact costs and performance. Based on this and with input from my Leadership Team, I approved an upward lift of 10% to the company's short-term incentive program (bonus) plan for non-executive roles. This adjustment was acknowledgment of the agility and resiliency of our employees and another way we used a values-based framework and decision model to support a good outcome.

With team members working remotely for sustained periods of time, employee wellbeing and mental health was paramount. Our Health and Safety team put together leader training focused on monitoring wellbeing and improving leadership skills in a hybrid work environment. The training was rolled out in April of 2021. We are also working to establish team norms that will help protect remote workers from burnout and the blurred boundaries between work and home.

We continue to learn. Circumstances continue to evolve, and so there are always lessons to glean. The devastation of the pandemic is irrefutable; the grievous loss and heartbreak in our employee base and across the world is real. However, the Covid-19 pandemic has been a catalyst for some positive change in how and where people work. It has also demonstrated how successful leaders can be if they leverage values-based decision-making frameworks, stay aligned and work to find the opportunity in every challenge.

Current Day and Wave III - July 2021 and Beyond

The post-Covid-19 world is still a vision. While vaccinations are now, thankfully, being distributed across the world, the pace cannot keep up with the need. Lives are still being lost. The logistics of vaccine distribution in some countries are difficult. Estimates to reach herd immunity stretch to years into the future, suggesting more heartbreak is ahead before the pandemic is truly behind us. Still, our leaders, team members and the world are embracing a new normal. Some of the challenges that face us are the same, but new ones have emerged: Operating in an environment of ongoing outbreaks, managing in a hybrid environment, supporting mental wellbeing of our workforce, and attracting and retaining talent in a "work-from-anywhere" world—these are all new challenges for not only Newmont, but leaders around the world.

Wave III will focus on new ways of working, ones that are sustainable and help enhance the diversity and talent pool of our global workforce. Still, there are many questions to answer: *How do we create an inclusive environment for all? How do we ensure we bring everyone along in a changing environment? What will need to change from a leadership perspective? What kind of training and technology will be needed?* These are the sort of critical issues we are thinking about and the impact of the decisions to solve for them will have a significant impact on the future culture of our organization.

Employee Support

At our corporate office in Denver, when team members return to the office, they will return to a new building. During the pandemic year, in a planned office move, we relocated our headquarters. However, not only the office has changed; our leaders, along with others worldwide have made the decision to downsize the office footprint, saving millions of dollars a year in office space, and also allowing employees flexibility in work location to suit the tasks they are doing and balance home and work commitments. Not everyone has embraced this approach. While the approach has gained traction with some, the cultural change of giving up a desk is significant. Many like creating a work space that is personal, and many are wondering where they will put their family photos and favorite coffee cup without a permanent space of their own.

We continue to seek feedback and will continue to adjust work environments to ensure employees are comfortable and connected where ever their work location is. One thing is certain: Newmont leaders will continue to communicate clearly, manage expectations and change as they discover different and more effective ways to work and lead.

Community Support

Our commitment to the community is unwavering. As of March 2021, over $11 million dollars of the original $20 million has been committed or spent to fund Covid-19 response and provide community support where it is needed most. To that point, over half of the spend to date has been distributed in Latin America, where lack of infrastructure and resources has compounded the devastating impact of the virus and hinders rapid distribution of the vaccine. Still, as vaccines are administered across the world, the hope is that it will ultimately slow or prevent a fourth wave of the virus. We will continue to use data models to predict and be prepared for any further impact to our people, operating sites or regions. Regional efforts to support Covid-19 relief and invest in our host communities will continue even after the Community Support Fund has been fully distributed. Newmont has always partnered with its local communities and governments to champion the people who work and live in the areas surrounding our operations. It is our purpose—to create value and improve lives through our work, and virus or not, that endeavor is resolute.

Operations

Our operations continue to evolve with a focus on excellence, agility and continuous improvement. Introducing Covid-19 safety measures were a necessary step for businesses globally, but with a strong safety culture in place, this transition was effectively made by our Newmont team. As we navigate the third wave and an unknown future, we will continue to evolve and refine how we work. With the proven ability to work remotely for some roles, I expect that our approach to business travel, role relocations and expatriate roles will change. We will continue to leverage technology, learning and expanding on what works, building new skills and capabilities in our systems and teams. With autonomous trucks currently being commissioned at Boddington in Australia and an electric mine at Borden, we are already finding ways to make gold production safer, while enhancing productivity and extending mine life. The lessons from Covid on what work can be done virtually, how many roles are truly needed full time at an operation, and how leaders can more effectively collaborate in a global company to overcome challenges will only enhance our strength going forward. The ability to source "virtual' talent in a global market has big implications for diversity targets and the future strength of teams and solutions. The challenges of the Covid-19 pandemic are not for naught; we will capitalize on every opportunity and use the lessons to build a better business.

"I look back at how our teams have managed through the pandemic with a great deal of pride," comments Rob Atkinson, my EVP and Chief Operating Officer. "I think we have all surprised ourselves by what we have been able to do. The resilience, willingness to accept very significant change and the care shown for each other and our host communities has been absolutely first class. Very proud to be part of the Newmont team!"

Conclusion and Lessons learned

The Covid-19 pandemic changed the world. As of this writing, there have been over three-million deaths from the virus. The world is reeling, grieving and forever altered. At Newmont, our response to the virus accelerated the cultural change curve toward new ways of working that are safer, more effective and will enhance productivity. There have been real challenges to overcome. The risk to people and operations was real; yet I believe our leadership approach served our team well. We have led our people through the worst of the pandemic and emerged stronger with best practices that Newmont will take into the future.

On this journey, the framework I utilized with my leadership team was simple. Its themes and lessons include::

- The importance of anchoring all decisions and actions in a common understanding of the context and clarity of purpose
- Leveraging a set of guiding principles that helped filter decision making for the leadership teams across the company
- Utilizing a Wave framework to reduce complexity and dismantle the complex, unpredictable nature of the crisis into manageable timeframes: To control what we could in the present moment and anticipate the best next steps through modeling data in future Waves
- Creating an environment in which leaders are seeking ongoing feedback from their teams and acting on it.
- Leveraging technology to enhance effectiveness
- Managing through uncertainty with transparent, honest and consistent communication
- Acknowledging external context, grounding decisions in a larger perspective
- Embracing a pragmatic, agile approach and learning focus; a willingness to evolve
- Monitoring individual and organizational wellbeing and taking strategic action to preserve both

- Recognizing that the decisions taken in responding to the pandemic were going to have a lasting impact on the culture of the organization and that it was essential that the long term sustainable health of the business was far more important than the short term response
- Accepting that sometimes impact to business is unavoidable, but the leadership and team member response to any given challenge can unearth an unforeseen upside

At Newmont, the events of Covid have been a catalyst for transformation and positive evolution of culture. This is not to discount the catastrophic global losses of the pandemic—to life, businesses, livelihood. We have lost team members and everyone feels the very real grief and weight of the pandemic; some of these will echo always. However, our ability to effectively navigate these events does not negate the realities, but instead helps redeem them. We have used these challenges to build a better future.

After one-hundred years, Newmont is still new, still learning and growing. The two years preceding the pandemic brought events including a spin off of the Nevada operations as part of a joint-venture with Barrick and the addition of five new operations resulting from the acquisition of Goldcorp. At its essence, the pandemic was a catalyst to shape culture in an accelerated integration process. Our deliberate leadership response helped ensure that the events were used to bring together Newmont's workforce of almost thirty thousand people, aligning everyone in a common purpose.

Newmont is emerging stronger than ever and this will not only benefit our workforce, but our host communities and surrounding economies. The ripple impacts are vast. We have demonstrated resilience; our team members feel supported and have seen our values in action. Commitment and productivity are high and financials are strong. My leadership team has defined a roadmap through challenge anchored in systems thinking and values-driven leadership. As the world slowly recovers and lives and businesses are restored, we continue to look forward. Hopefully we will not have to navigate such a crisis again, but if we do, we will be ready.

9

How some Australian businesses managed the challenge

WRITTEN BY GEOFF MCGILL, GRAEME
MITCHELL AND ROB CHASTON

Introduction and Context

This chapter reviews responses to the Pandemic based on 10 business case studies ranging from a small family enterprise to a well-established multinational. It reviews what was done by the leaders of the business and how it was done using the SLT as the framework for analysis. It identifies common critical issues that had to be resolved if the business was to survive and any issues specific or unique to that undertaking. The sample studied is small and not generally representative, as all the businesses managed to survive but the pathways to that outcome were as varied as the organisations themselves.

Purpose

To use the Systems Leadership framework and models to review how a range of businesses responded to the challenges of the Covid-19 pandemic.

The businesses

The leaders of the selected businesses were interviewed and asked to respond to a series of pre-determined questions. The questions are detailed at the end of this chapter.

What follows here is a brief background about the businesses and some of the positive and negatives experiences they encountered during the period reviewed. It should be noted that subsequent to the interviews Victoria succumbed to a second wave of the virus and underwent a severe shutdown across the greater Metropolitan area. At the time of writing, two businesses particularly affected by the second shutdown are to be interviewed again and included in a postscript to the chapter.

Business A

This business is located in regional NSW, was established 10 years ago and is run by 4 partners.

Its principal activity is the operation of gyms and fitness centres located at three sites. Prior to closing down, it employed 5 full-time staff and 40 casuals. Of these the 5 full-timers and 13 of the casuals qualified for Australian Government JobKeeper Payment.

Management focused on communication to staff and customers, financial issues including cost minimization, generation of alternate income and facility maintenance. While they had adequate cash reserves their early focus was on the need to preserve this buffer. Rent negotiation took place and communication with suppliers and creditors was another early target. Their banker was very supportive.

They also maintained contact with their industry association. Members could sign in for Covid updates to understand the public health constraints applying and the approach followed across the industry. The role of the association was viewed positively, and this feedback is consistent with the experience of other entities particularly the hotels interviewed. The role of these associations augmenting the organisational capability of members is discussed later in this Chapter.

Other concerns included the quality of communication to staff and customers particularly in the face of uncertainty of the length of shutdown. Anxiety levels were high. While only a relatively small business, given the need to integrate systems across 3 operating sites, the work of the leader involved tasks of 4 complexity.

Business B

Located in Regional Victoria at an iconic location this business is a single operation hotel which has been operated by the owners for 8 years. A husband and wife team they have worked together for 14 years. The business was well known and established prior to the initial shut down.

Closure of the business, with 24 hours' notice was a shock for all concerned. Some 40 staff were stood down, cash flow ceased, and they had to raise significant debt, stock losses occurred and communication with staff after closure was problematic. Individual staff members reported high levels of stress, particularly as the period of closure extended.

Owners reported that their bank was slow to provide support, but their beer supplier was very helpful by taking back unused stock. Some staff qualified for JobKeeper and few were utilized in a home delivery service. This service enabled them to maintain a modest level of service to customers. Where possible, the owners shared this work around.

Their accountant and the Australian Hotels Association were key to managing the issues that arose.

Owners changed their mode of operating when allowed to reopen and customers are enjoying a new style of hospitality and service in a social distancing environment. But indoor capacity is more restricted and outdoor drinking and dining is subject to the vagaries of the weather.

For the owners the biggest issue for them was fear of the unknown and particularly the perceived risk of a second lockdown, which did subsequently take place.

As an independently owned hotel the owner operators must integrate technical, commercial and social systems specific to the business. Ongoing operational success required leadership work of minimum 4 complexity.

Business C

Also located in regional Victoria this husband and wife team have run a single hotel for 12 years and have many years prior experience running hotels in the district. They report the business as being well established with a good customer base.

On closure, at 24 hours' notice, finance became an immediate issue as annual turnover of $1.5 m became zero, a stock loss of $70,000 materialised and there was a need for the owners to quickly draw on business reserves, personal cash and family finances to keep their heads above water. Some suppliers were very helpful while at least one (a significant public company) threatened legal action which may have been illegal in the circumstances. Banks and insurance companies were said to be unhelpful.

The business had 8 fulltime staff and 16 casuals as well as cleaners and security people. In order to maintain their insurance, the owners also became the security guards during the lockdown.

While staff were paid their entitlements and JobKeeper was eventually used in some cases, all personnel were said to be very anxious and the owners were most concerned about the mental health of one person in particular.

Owners commented positively about JobKeeper, the $10,000 BAS credit scheme, support from family and friends as well as advice from their accountant and the AHA.

Their major concern during closure was "staying afloat and would we be able to resume and staying sane." This is another example of the owners dealing with tasks of 4 complexity.

Business D

Based in regional Victoria, this case is a physiotherapy practice, one of two covered in the study.

This owner operated his business, as an essential service, did not have to close down but was required to cease face to face work because of social distancing and transitioned to online consultation.

As with so many other businesses its cashflow was badly affected and consultations dropped from 65 sessions a week to 10. The owner focussed on cost reduction and amongst other things managed a 50% rent reduction. He was in the fortunate position of having financial resources to cover 6-8 months of fixed business and personal commitments.

One of his main concerns was patient loyalty and the risk of them finding other options for treatment. He took to e-book and social media to maintain contact with his patient list.

He also had four sub-contractors and deployed an online assessment tool (new system) for them to check in with their patients. Fortunately, both the owner and the sub-contractors were able to access JobKeeper. He reported mixed results from the online initiative and also reported that the contractors were very much reliant on him coming up with ideas and strategies. He felt he was "hand holding".

On reflection he believed he could/should have done a better job of checking in with clients. Having said that he thinks customer loyalty is still strong.

The financial resources available to the owner enabled continued operation but with a new system of online patient assessment. Normally, a physiotherapy practice works within a range of prescribed protocols and systems, diagnosis of cases within a system involving tasks of 2 complexity.

The systems design work required for online patient assessment suggests work of minimum 3 complexity. Face to face consultations have now resumed, and the practice now operates both systems.

Business E

This business, also located in regional Victoria, is an owner operated café/coffee shop.

At lockdown the owner moved to a take-away only operation with apparent success, as his cashflow wasn't impacted. They sold the same number of coffees, food income reduced somewhat but he let some staff go and the net result was a reduction in overheads by 25%. Casuals were let go but the remaining 5 staff were able to stay on.

While suppliers continued to operate some things were harder to source, particularly takeaway cups and disposable gloves. The owner was able to take advantage of the government's offer of BAS credits totalling $20,000 and qualified for a government small business grant of $10,000 which he applied for online.

All in all it seems this business owner managed to change the way he operates without difficulty and reports that he is doing the same but with less work and fewer hours. He thinks it is hard to see himself reverting to longer hours and having to go back to a larger selection of food and other services or products. That said there is the critical issue of "what if my customers want me to go back to being able to provide the pre-existing levels of product and service once the trading environment normalizes?"

This small business owner operator has responded well to the critical issues arising. The development of takeaway arguably involved the design of a single field system, that is work of 3 complexity. He is reluctant to revert back to the previous operating model, involving longer hours of work which would need to integrate with a successful take away system with less hours of work.

Business F

Having been in operation for 22 years this company, a small manufacturer of metal products, is owned by one person. While not required to stop trading, turnover in the first two weeks of lockdown dropped by 90% but more than recovered after that due to the introduction of a new Covid-19 pandemic related product.

The company employed 9 people and the owner's key driver was to focus on keeping everyone in a job. He initially cut back hours and also ceased overtime. He believes that because of good communication, via staff meetings, staff reacted surprisingly well with the end result that none were significantly negatively impacted.

Financially the business was not badly affected with some costs reduced and also backup by way of a $100,000 SME loan as a buffer against unforeseen costs or unexpected turnover reduction. Banks were co-operative and supportive, and any issues were resolved. The owner was also able to successfully apply for JobKeeper and took advantage of the $10,000 BAS credit.

Supplier liaison was a high priority and creditors were kept informed about the status of their accounts.

On review, the owner indicated one of his greatest challenges revolved around managing his own stress and that of his staff as well as keeping morale high. Another challenge was dealing with an increased volume of sales while suppliers were struggling to meet the demand for an increase in orders from the company. Juggling cashflow was also an issue.

On a positive note, a new product that was Covid relevant was designed and developed in 10 days. The owner believes he has "had an incredibly positive business experience during Covid." He intends to increase his focus on online sales and through dealers rather than relying exclusively on showroom walk ins.

He also believes that his personal relationships with his employees has been strengthened during the period.

The owner led the development and marketing of a new product suited to the environment of Covid-19 which successfully integrated into the existing business with increased sales. Through personal persistence he was also to clarify with the regulator an apparent and widely assumed constraint against continued operations and avoid closure during the lockdown. This involved work of 4 minimum complexity. The successful management of the external regulatory environment to secure continued operation suggests work of 5 complexity.

Business G

This business is a family owned chartered accountancy practice operating in two Victorian country towns and has been in operation for over 30 years.

As an essential business they have continued operation from home and indeed have seen their business grow through the pandemic. They described escalation of demand for their services as "frantic". Principal reasons are said to be the value of their "business continuity tool" (a product developed by an accounting group they belong to) in the second quarter and subsequently, tax advice work and the various government stimulus initiatives.

They identified major issues around managing mental health and retaining clients particularly those based in Melbourne. Another issue of note is the fact that there is a growing need to have difficult conversations with clients who are struggling and who need to face the fact that insolvency laws are back in play.

Apart from a receptionist, their 13 employees have been retained and all are working from home. Regular meetings with staff and clients take place via Zoom or Microsoft Teams. These meetings have also been valuable in order to address internal staff concerns and uncertainty about job security. In addition, the partners have been speaking to individual staff members weekly.

Challenges ahead include developing staff training for people working from home particularly as some report that they feel as if they are stagnating. This takes on increased significance as the partners believe that most people will continue to work from home in the future.

Finally, the partners feel as if their work as leaders has become tougher because of the need to create a sustainable and positive workplace where their team is spread far and wide and may not get together frequently as a group.

As an essential business, shut down was not required. Business demands in fact increased and the business continuity tool they had previously developed worked well - evidence of work of minimum 3 complexity. However, working from home is a major system change and likely to be required over the long term. Integration of this change into the overall business model is essential and demonstrates work of 4 complexity.

Business H

Also, in the health care industry, this business is located in country regional Victoria. It operates as a company with two principal owners. The business employs 8 other people.

The physical practice comprises a number of consulting rooms, a small gym and also conducts hydrotherapy classes at a shared facility on a sessional basis for about 6 hours a week. While the practice is classed as an essential service hydrotherapy classes were discontinued but resumed in late 2020. Usually the gym operation accommodated five clients and to manage social distancing this was reduced to two.

Analysis of financial data showed that the business qualified for Job-Keeper and their accountant dealt with the application. They also qualified for a Victorian government grant for small business of $10,000. A rent reduction of 10% was agreed to and the principal owners did not draw down salaries and relied on JobKeeper payments.

No staff members were stood down but one, because of age, decided not to work during the shutdown periods.

Due to changes needed to work arrangements the office practice manager expressed concerns about the fairness of these changes which resulted in working longer hours. The sense of unfairness was exacerbated by the fact that some members of staff were paid more under Job-Keeper than they were in normal circumstances. Some adjustment in practice was made by additional hours on a voluntary basis by the Job-keeper recipient.

Efforts were also made by the partners to ensure that they success-fully managed other staff issues including staff dealing with home schooling and stress factors arising on the home front.

Like the other physiotherapy practice, the principals and profes-sional staff, work within a range of prescribed protocols and systems and the business was not required to shut down. Nonetheless some systems design work to offer online consultations and to adjust the operation of the JobKeeper was required, suggesting the Professional Practice leader was engaged in work of minimum 3 complexity.

Business I

Based in metropolitan Sydney this business operates 14 hotels prin-cipally in the inner and outer west of the metropolitan area. The busi-ness was established in 1987 and the current CEO has been in role since 2013. While operating under a corporate umbrella it is essentially a fam-ily owned and run organization.

In accordance with government Covid rules the business was shut down in late March with limited notice given by the authorities.

While a limited cashflow was maintained through the operation of bottle shops at some sites income from liquor and gaming ceased result-ing in a 98% decrease in revenue and a negative cashflow to follow. The immediate principal concern was financial, but their bankers quickly waived financial covenants and deferred interest payments "at least until we run out of money". Further backup liquidity arrangement were put in place. NSW government also deferred payment of the Gaming tax.

Early focus by the management team was on compliance with gov-ernment Covid requirements.

At the time of closure, the business had 24 fulltime employees, 156 casuals and a small Head Office team. By reopening they had only lost 5% of their casuals to other employment.

The CEO could see that communication to all staff needed to come from him for message consistency. The need to shut down quickly exposed shortcomings in the businesses capacity to communicate to all staff efficiently as well as problems with the rostering and payroll systems. A review across the systems of the operation was put in place quite quickly after shutdown occurred and its scope has expanded since.

Many of the stood down staff qualified for JobKeeper which the CEO said was enormously helpful. His underlying message to staff was "While we are solvent you have a job."

Apart from dealing with financial and social issues ongoing work revolved around supplier liaison, bringing forward some property maintenance and liaising with government including the Liquor Licensing Court and The Gaming Authority. Urgent work was also required to reconfigure gaming areas to achieve the required social distancing. At reopening they had 95% of their machines operating.

CEO was also particularly complimentary about the overarching role the AHA played in the sector.

According to the CEO he and his executive team actively identified critical issues and he involved them and others in assessing solutions. By the time of reopening the business had sound plans in place and resumption of trading was well strategised and implemented.

While essentially family owned, the corporate structure governing operations across 14 hotels requires close integration of the commercial, social and technical systems common across those sites. This clearly work of minimum 4 complexity. In addition, the CEO must lead work with external regulatory and commercial entities in order that the business is self-sustaining in its environment. This is work of 5 complexity.

Business J

This business is a publicly listed company on the ASX. It is in the food manufacturing industry and is therefore classified as an essential business. Based in Sydney it operates businesses in Australia, New Zealand, China, the UK and the USA.

The CEO retired in July 2018 having taken up his role 8 years earlier. His successor resigned after a short tenure and the former CEO returned to the business until a permanent replacement could take up duty, expected by the end of 2020.

In the first quarter of 2020 as the pandemic took hold the company saw a significant upward sales trend while pantry stocking (panic buying) took place around the world. In the following quarter sales settled back to normal levels. The company's cashflow fluctuation in that 6 months was effectively neutral.

Financial risks aside, management focussed on processing risks particularly in Australia and NZ. Further attention was given to supply chain risk and transport risk. Mitigants for all identified risks were put in place and continue to be closely monitored. In other words, the company identified critical issues, sought appropriate contributions and ideas and decided on a clear plan to manage the business in a volatile environment.

Staff numbers in Australia approximate 300 and no stand downs have occurred. Social distancing rules were implemented and rigorously monitored. A senior person was appointed to give heightened focus to O H and S matters.

Early in the piece, communication to all staff at all sites emanated from HO to ensure consistency of message on a daily basis. The Microsoft Teams system was established for ease of communication to staff, suppliers, customers and other stakeholders in all countries where they have operations. Indeed, the CEO believes that a side benefit of the crisis has been improved staff engagement.

On reflection, the CEO felt his biggest challenge was to maintain his own visibility with staff generally but also his executive team and HO personnel many of whom worked from home. He believes the effort put in to doing so paid dividends for a business facing the same challenges as businesses of all shapes and size.

The overseas sites managed by the CEO are, with one exception, confined to marketing and sales but operate in very different cultures. The role involves tasks of 5 complexity.

"Well that was interesting!"

Although only a small sample of businesses, it may be of use to consider how well these businesses fared when looked at against the Team Leader and Team Member steps [1].

The Context in which these businesses unexpectedly and rapidly found themselves should have been well understood by the Team Leaders at the time albeit for many of them their immediate reaction may well have been disbelief, panic, anxiety and fear. Hopefully their reactions were not so negative that individually they could not effectively and coherently discuss the situation with their team members.

At this point perhaps it is useful to consider what is the Purpose of a business?

What follows is not meant to supplant what individual businesses and organisations have clearly enunciated as their purpose in a healthy and competitive environment in their sector of operation.

Indeed, in the context of the Covid-19 pandemic it may be hypothesized that many businesses found the need to refocus from the purpose of sustaining the operation of the business over the longer term to something like "To maintain the business in as healthy a state as is possible so as to survive the Covid-19 pandemic".

While Constraints within which the teams are working in the normal course should be well known, it could well be that in the very early Covid context fresh constraints were being put in place by governments, regulators and the like which were, by sheer volume, adding to the complexity of work at the coal face in an environment which was potentially overwhelming for many people involved at different levels in the business.

Having understood the changed context and purpose in which so many businesses found themselves, the next step for them should have been to identify the Critical Issues which threatens the purpose. Sometimes described as "showstoppers" we describe them as "what-ifs" and address them with "how-tos."

According to Systems Leadership (2nd Ed chapter 3) Domains of Work are categorised into three key areas. The three fundamental domains are Social, Technical and Commercial. These domains are not a ranking of importance, but it needs to be well understood that organisations cannot function effectively unless it is clear how the work is done in each domain and how it interacts with the two other interdependent domains.

In considering the identification of critical issues we have chosen to identify them within the domains referred to here. This is not intended to be an exhaustive list of "showstoppers" but is illustrative of the thinking work that, in the circumstances, needs to be done by all businesses as a Plan is developed and decided upon to achieve the Purpose. That is, these were common critical issues that had to be resolved by all businesses studied in the sample.

Social

How to:

- communicate with staff initially, and ongoing?
- communicate with financiers and banks?
- communicate with stakeholders such as investors and shareholders?
- communicate with suppliers?
- manage staff members who are faced with job loss?
- appropriately support and /or source professional support for individual staff members facing financial or mental health issues?
- access government support initiatives such as Job Keeper?

- staff members take their final payments and simply leave the business?
- staff members want to immediately take their outstanding annual and long service leave immediately and on full pay?

Commercial
How to:

- manage finances including banks and creditors?
- collect outstanding debtors?
- plan around the possibility of mandated long term closure?
- plan for reopening?
- operate the business within Covid rules for my sector?
- manage expenses and reduce daily costs to a manageable level?
- locate/establish/manage/build relationships with industry lobby bodies and industry support organisations in order to understand and obtain advice on issues arising in the wider industry context?

What if:

- financiers cannot or are unwilling to provide support?
- our insurers raise obstacles to claims?
- suppliers want unpaid stock returned?
- debtors are not in a position to meet their obligations?
- key suppliers fail?
- we as the business owners/leaders feel we do not have the capability to manage increasing complexity in the current operational context?
- governments or reports on government policy don't provide consistent, correct and up to date information?

Technical:

How to:

- ensure business continuity during shutdown?

What if:

- our internal systems such of accounting, payroll, sales manage-ment, stock control etc. fail and we cannot source the expertise to recover them?
- production systems breakdown?

The list of critical issues is not exhaustive and the formulation of the issue in the language of critical issues by those interviewed was often im-plicit rather explicit. But even with this small sample, these issues were likely to be representative of the critical issues faced commonly across hundreds of Australian workplaces.

Tools of Leadership and Cultural Change

One of the challenges a business faces at any time is to create and maintain its desired workplace culture. In times of crisis this becomes even more important as significant issues will arise from the increasingly complex operating business environment that will 'test' both the capa-bility of the organisation and its leaders.

Each of the businesses in this report were faced with this dilemma and the following is an analysis using Systems Leadership Theory (SLT) to provide insights into. how three of those organisations dealt with this challenge. SLT has developed as an integrated theory of organiza-tion and leadership behaviour based on observations of behaviour in many different organisations over many decades. Models and tools have been developed to aid leaders in understanding and shaping the culture of their organisation. But successful leadership does not depend on the leaders having a detailed understanding of the theory. Rather in the context of these case studies, SLT helps to explain and understand the observed behaviour and outcomes and suggest a methodology that can be successfully repeated by leaders in a variety of different circumstances arising in the future. In other words, the application of the methodology is a basis for making predictions about the pathways most likely to achieve the purpose of the organisation.

The work of a leader is to create, maintain and improve the culture of a group of people so that they achieve objectives and continue to do so over time. As the model below depicts this requires an understanding by the leader of the current culture, reflected in the current mythologies (the assumptions and beliefs people hold) and a vision of the desired culture, including the positive aspects of the current culture that should be retained but also the changes that the leader and people of the organisation would like in terms of the behaviours and their experience of working in the organisation.

The model also depicts the change process through the creation of dissonance (the experience that something different and unpredicted is happening which isn't going away as shown in consistent and persistent leadership) and the embedding of that change using the tools of leadership - systems, symbols and leadership behaviour to sustain cultural change by creating new desired mythologies and reinforcing the positive mythologies of the current culture. This model will be used to discuss the three business case studies selected for further analysis.

Culture Change

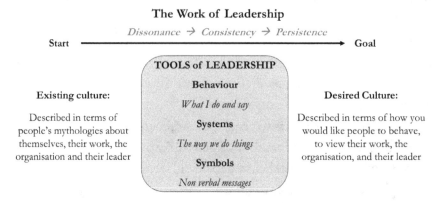

The Work of Leadership

Dissonance → Consistency → Persistence

Start ────────────────────────────→ Goal

TOOLS of LEADERSHIP

Behaviour

What I do and say

Systems

The way we do things

Symbols

Non verbal messages

Existing culture:

Described in terms of people's mythologies about themselves, their work, the organisation and their leader

Desired Culture:

Described in terms of how you would like people to behave, to view their work, the organisation, and their leader

Systems Leadership: Creating Positive Organisations. 2nd Edition. Ian Macdonald, Catherine Burke and Karl Stewart. Routledge 2018

1.   *Business F*

Current and Desired Culture

The CEO of 'Business F' described his company as having a positive and productive culture in which people flourished and were able to reach their potential, and that innovation was the backbone of their growth path. Systems Leadership Theory (SLT) proposes that for a business to create its desired culture it does so by using the 'tools of leadership' - systems, symbols and behaviour. These tools are used to implement effective work and people systems, with supportive positive workplace symbols and leadership behaviour which is experienced by the people of the organization on the positive side of the Values Continua. (see below)

The challenge for him was in maintaining this positive culture in an operating environment that, given the severity of the second lockdown restrictions being implemented by the state government, posed a real risk that the business would have to close. A major change in the business operating model and systems was required to avoid this outcome.

How this was done would impact positively or negatively on the current culture through the judgments people made against the Values Continua.

His initial response to the potential shutdown of his business as a result of the "second wave" of the novel coronavirus, was that his business did not seem to meet the 'essential service' criteria as reported in media reports. But "What if this information was not correct? His reaction was twofold, first, he had been given contrary advice about the definition of 'essential services' and pursued the matter through "Business Victoria" (see detail below), the State Government department that provided support and information to businesses operating in Victoria, to clarify whether his business was a 'permitted work premises" (the terminology used by government to classify businesses allowed to continue operations). This is a very important point, as initial government advice as reported by mainstream media, led to the misunderstanding that most businesses would have to close. However, upon investigation, this was not the case. In fact, government was encouraging manufacturing businesses to remain open, but that was not the 'messaging' in most media reports. In initial response to this, as well as the dip in sales, the CEO did in fact reduce hours of work for one week, before clarifying that his was a "permitted business".

Values Continua

Trustworthy	⟵———————⟶	Untrustworthy
Loving	⟵———————⟶	Unloving
Honest	⟵———————⟶	Dishonest
Fair	⟵———————⟶	Unfair
Courageous	⟵———————⟶	Cowardly
Respectful / Dignifying	⟵———————⟶	Disrespectful / Undignifying

Systems Leadership: Creating Positive Organisations. 2nd Edition. Ian Macdonald, Catherine Burke and Karl Stewart. Routledge 2018

The process

1. Owner was advised by a customer that the Govt's classification of "Steel Fabricated Products" had been shifted to the Manufacturing Sector's "Permitted Work Premises"
2. On investigation it was learnt that the Australian Steel Industry (via their website) had announced that their last minute lobbying resulted in the above change occurring just hours earlier.
3. According to the "Permitted Work Premises" list (effective 5 August) on DHHS website, they could most likely continue to manufacture the Sanitiser Stands but uncertain about normal products.
4. He contacted Business Victoria and explained circumstances and confirmed, and recorded, that because of the Sanitiser Stands product they could continue to manufacture normal products alongside the stands. They said that the Vic Govt wanted manufacturing to continue wherever possible and that if a manufacturer was already making an "essential item" they had the right to use their manufacturing capacity for their regular (non-essential) products at the same time.
5. Thus, because of the Sanitiser Stands, Business F was classified as "Permitted Work Premises" but of concern was the statement "the business cannot operate on-site for any other purpose" was still showing on the Business Victoria information as of August 7. Despite this, Business Victoria assured them they were 100% OK to manufacture normal products.

Second, innovation was very much a part of this business' culture and thus was a natural response to the difficulties facing them. In this case, that response was to replace lost sales with a new product. The idea of manufacturing hand-sanitizer stands came from the spouse of an employee; it was considered by the business' Product Development Team and progressed from concept to final product within ten days. By relying on their core organisational capabilities, their systems and positive leadership, the CEO kept people fully employed, with the consequence that he kept the current culture in place. This also affirmed the perception of his leadership i.e. he demonstrated love, was honest, treated his people with dignity, was prepared to take a risk for them (courage) and his business, continued to be someone they trusted and someone who treated everyone the same e.g. cut in hours (fairness).

Given the integrated nature of SLT, the above example touches on a number of areas but primarily the Cultural Change Model (including of course the Tools of Leadership), Levels of Work, the Team Process Model, the Values Continua, the Task Assignment Model, the Three Questions and Systems Design work. As explained above, the CEO used a system (recently designed) – called "Product Development" – to "turn intention into reality". It is important to note that in small businesses many of the "20 systems design questions" are not, by process, asked or directly addressed, but engagement with these issues of system design is evident in the successful work that was done. The SLT models help reveal common elements of a productive pathway that can potentially be repeated. This was discussed in more detail in the Chapter 2, The "Ruby Princess" – the complexity of systems design. The system owner was the CEO, and the Designers/Users were the Production Manager, the Sales Administrator and the CEO. They did identify the context and purpose of the system, explained how the system worked along with accountabilities and authorities, and there were controls and audit in place. There was an awareness and accommodation of interacting systems such as design, manufacture, procurement and delivery without it being documented. The system was cost effective, productive and allowed appropriate exercise of discretion.

The design for the hand-sanitiser stand was reviewed along with relevant supplier, costings and forecast sales information. With the CEO being part of this group, authority to proceed was not an obstacle, although the decision to proceed was not unanimous. The next steps involved using existing manufacturing processes to create a 'pilot' product (which would be used as a display model) and using the marketing system to begin promoting the stand to local markets. The key point here is that existing systems were robust enough to allow the product to be manufactured, marketed and sold within a very short space of time. Although sales for their core products quickly rebounded, they had in fact created a new product for a new market, which contributed to removing the stress of job loss and income as well as dealing with the spike in complexity created by federal and state governments' responses to the pandemic.

In terms of "Levels of Work", the CEO was required to undertake work "where things may not be as they appear" (Level 4) and in which "guiding the Business through the conflicts caused by the impact of the Business on the environment and the modification of the Business to accommodate the changes necessary to have the Business prosper in that environment" (Level 5) (Macdonald 2018). This was demonstrated through pursuing the government for an accurate interpretation of what a "permitted workplace" meant, instead of accepting the common interpretation, and then adapting to the changed business environment by introducing a product that was required by government restrictions.

From a team process perspective, and again without the CEO being cognizant of that process, many of the team leader behaviours and some traps can be identified in what happened with the business. The context and purpose of the task were clear i.e. government restrictions indicated that the business would not be allowed to continue operations and the purpose was to keep it open. Constraints were not clear i.e. government restrictions, an issue addressed by the CEO and described above. Identifying critical issues was a natural rather than process step and were to a significant extent actions to address these issues that formed the basis of the plan e.g. what if the business was not a "permitted workplace"? How to keep people employed? The CEO actively sought contributions from all employees and advisers and the plan that was decided reflected the identified critical issues i.e. changing hours of work, clarifying government restrictions and developing a replacement product. Different tasks were assigned and monitored (the CEO was familiar with the task assignment model) e.g. development and sales of the new product. Coaching and supporting his people was something the CEO did as a matter of course and this was demonstrated through the sale of the hand-sanitiser stand by being at the front-line in engaging with prospective businesses, instead of leaving that work to his staff. Review of the task (as a team process step[2]) to stay operational was not a deliberate step, although in meetings with their business advisers the plan was discussed.

Symbolically, the above actions by the CEO reinforced the positive perceptions of his leadership particularly his persistence in clarifying the interpretation of his business as a 'permitted workplace' and expediting the development of a new product to replace lost sales. Last, the CEO's efforts helped him answer the third question "what is my future?"

2.   Business A

The initial challenge for Business A was around the critical issues of how to manage the loss of income and how to care for both employees and customers. The business relied on employing those with expertise and on repeat business. There was clarity around the constraints imposed by government's first lockdown restrictions which meant his business had to close, so the task for the CEO was how to limit the immediate financial impact (cash-burn) and how to maintain connection to employees and customers in anticipation of the business re-opening.

The CEO was familiar with SLT and deliberately used some of the models to assist him in his work e.g. in structuring his communications with employees and customers he used the values continua (see figure above) to predict possible responses to his messages and proposed business changes, in order to prepare for questions from them. This didn't necessarily change what he had to say but helped him prepare potential responses. He remarked that this work definitely helped in creating positive communications and in keeping connected to these key people.

The second observation is that the CEO found that he needed to change the work he was doing in order to address the survival of the business. This involved understanding and adapting to the important environmental changes by addressing the commercial aspect of his business. He did this by minimising costs, generating new income via their online store, selling future passes including life membership, communicating with customers, maintaining facilities and undertaking improvements where possible. As with the previous example in Business F, he also found himself having to undertake tasks of higher complexity as part of the work of his role (at Levels 4 and 5) in which it was important to take a company-wide view of his business, including understanding and responding to the wider operating environment, rather than just focusing on the issues arising at specific locations. This also included taking a more prominent role with the Board and initiating actions and solutions rather than just reporting problems to them. He successfully completed this work. He said the biggest 'take-away' for him from the business experience of the pandemic was that he needed to continue operating at the level his role required.

During the Pandemic tasks of 5 complexity arose for Businesses A and F. The leaders concerned were able to deal with the spike in complexity posed by the Pandemic, but both can anticipate that if a growth trajectory is to be maintained tasks of this complexity will become more common if not an already a dominate part of the work of the role. Figure below depicts a hypothetical position for at role at Level 4. Work at complexity 5 can arise and may not always be formally assigned The Pandemic is not over, and the risks of restrictions being reimposed in Australia is constant. In these two cases the capability to manage this level of complexity was evident but the wider critical issue posed by Covid-19 is "what if the availability of capability to deal with the policy and systems challenges we face is not sufficient in the current cohort of political and business leaders?"

Task Complexity

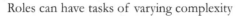

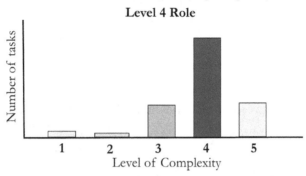

Roles can have tasks of varying complexity

Level 4 Role

Systems Leadership: Creating Positive Organisations. 2nd Edition. Ian Macdonald, Catherine Burke and Karl Stewart. Routledge 2018

From an SLT perspective, and using the cultural change model, the CEO recognised that the current culture was one he wanted to retain. It contributed to a positive and productive workplace for owners, employees and customers, and it supported a business that had a pattern of positive growth and financial return. Although he knew the model, he did not deliberately use it, however his actions can be explained through the tools of leadership i.e. his demonstration of love for employees and customers through his communications and the positive symbolism in inviting employees he had previously terminated (they were not eligible for Job Keeper) and key customers to undertake tasks in the gyms that were greatly valued by them. This provided a connection to the facilities, the business and demonstrated that they were valued. In SLT terms, the CEO had asked, regarding those who did not qualify for JK "what can I do?", "how do they experience this?" and "how would they view this through the Values Continua?". As stated earlier he wanted to maintain the current culture, and this decision was consistent with that goal. It also was an opportunity for him to see how, using the Values Continua, two different groups judged his behaviour (positively as it turned out).

The CEO made clear that he was most proud of the work he undertook around the commercial and social aspects of the business, best demonstrated in the response to the re-opening of the facilities in July (once restrictions had eased) by staff that "it's awesome to be back".

3. Business E

This business is an owner operated café located in regional Victoria. In comparison to other businesses in this study, his challenges were relatively straight-forward. In response to the critical issues of "how to operate the business within Covid rules for my sector and how to manage expenses and reduce daily costs to a manageable level", he moved to a take-away business only and reduced levels of casual staff. As with other businesses, he had to respond to an immediately changed operating environment with few resources to support him. He also reduced operating hours which meant he had more time at home. He relied on the local Council for information about operating restrictions including social distancing and hygiene requirements, and only had 48 hours to change his business model to comply. He accessed some government support, but not Job Keeper, as his sales and income did not fall.

In SLT terms, this example helps illustrate the interaction of at least three aspects of the models i.e. domains of work which are present in varying degrees in work regardless of its level of complexity, systems design and levels of work complexity work complexity (See Chapter .... Ruby Princess for a more detailed discussion). The owner's initial response to the lockdown was a commercial consideration, "how to make up for the loss of revenue?" That also involved social dimension; it impacted on people. Technical dimensions relating to OHS were also involved especially relating to managing the risks of transmission of Covid-19. In relation to work complexity, the owner had to weigh up the impact of the government's restrictions on seating inside restaurants and cafés, and therefore on the number of staff he required. Moving the business to take-away coffees only, certainly involved increasing the output of take away system. – monitoring and diagnostic work within an existing system indicating work of 2 complexity. But when it became apparent that the second lockdown would soon end, and restrictions would be eased to allow table service, another choice arose.

The owner had to make a one-off decision between continuing with a successful take-away coffee business that could be run at less cost, with fewer staff and reduced operating hours, resulting in a better lifestyle balance for himself, versus a model where the customers had a choice to sit inside his cafe with table service, or take away. At the end of the day, he decided to continue operating but with take away likely to be a larger part of the business and therefore higher sales overall. He saw a risk, that he would actually lose some of a potentially larger customer base if resuming full operations was delayed (competitors were resuming normal operations too).

In the event, the owner continued to work within the system which he had originally designed, indicating work of 3 complexity but doing familiar doing tasks of 1 and 2 complexity. The question of whether the one-off decision described above was a trade-off decision, characteristic of work at level 4, remains open. Clearly it is not a regular feature of the work of the role, but the choice of a better lifestyle is something most small businesspeople would like to have!

The Role of Industry Associations and Organisation Capability

In a number of the cases studied industry associations have been called on to provide specialist advice to their members about managing the issues arising from the constraints imposed during the pandemic. Associations have also lobbied on behalf of members to ease those constraints when these were seen to causing economic distress to industry beyond what was required to protect public health requirements.

SLT defines the elements of individual capability as follows:

- Knowledge
- Technical Skills
- Social process Skills
- Mental processing ability
- Application - desire, energy and drive applied to work.[3]

Organisational capability can be seen as the sum of these components but the effective realization of that organisation capability is very much dependent on the culture of the organisation. Knowledge and technical skills in public health, including epidemiology and effective control of the transmission of highly infectious, is not the preserve of the typical business organization. In this context, however, industry associations provided an important resource helping to disseminate and distill key information on constraints to be observed and how work practices were being adapted in the sector to enable continued operations and obligations to be observed in the event of closure. In this way industry associations have augmented the current organisational capability of their members

Typically in Australia advice has been provided by industry associations on labour relation and OHS law and practice. More specialist and complex legal and commercial matters tend to be the province of professional law firms.

Only very large national and multinational organisations are likely to have the necessary in-house expertise to handle major changes in context affecting the technical, commercial and social domains of work in their organization. But even these big businesses have felt the need, when responding to the challenges posed Covid-19, to seek expert external advice from government agencies and international bodies.

Conclusion

The purpose in this Chapter was to use the Systems Leadership framework and models to review how a range of businesses responded to the challenges of the Covid-19 pandemic. A common purpose for was hypothesized for the 10 businesses reviewed - how to:

"Maintain the business in as healthy a state as is possible so as to survive the Covid-19 pandemic".

To achieve this, the typical critical issues that had to be confronted and resolved by the leaders and organisations concerned were identified and discussed. While critical issues were largely common, the pathway to resolution differed and was shaped by the context, and culture of the businesses concerned. Three cases were analysed in more detail using the tools and models of SLT. Our purpose was to explain and understand the observed behaviours of leaders and team members and the resulting outcomes against the common purpose proposed above. All of the entities reviewed did survive the pandemic and the leaders concerned except for case studies A and F had no prior knowledge or understanding of SLT.

The interview protocol was explicitly designed to allow discussion about domains of work (technical, social and commercial) but did not explicitly prompt the respondent to use the language or models of SLT. It was on the basis of the respondents' narrative that the authors assessed whether the steps taken by the leaders to achieve their purpose could be explained in terms of SLT.

We consider that objective has been achieved and there is nothing to suggest the methodology of SLT could not be successfully repeated by capable leaders to achieve their organisational purpose in a variety of different circumstances arising in the future. However, sample of organisations reviewed is small and the practical limitations of conducting face to face interviews during the public health constraints impose due to Covid-19 meant employees could not in most cases be interviewed.

In normal circumstances a more comprehensive organisational analysis, usually called a "systems and symbols audit, would be conducted which is then used to make predictions about the pathways most likely to achieve the purpose of the organisation.

Attachment 1

Business Questions – Covid-19 Leadership and Organisation Background

1. How long have you run the business?
2. What is the business structure?

Section 1. Initial Impact of Covid-19

1. **Business activity**
   - Did you have to stop trading? ...for how long?
   - What happened to your cash flow?
   - How did you manage the financial impact?
   - What problems were you most concerned about?
   - Were you able to make any plans and preparations?
2. **People**
   - How many people did you employ at the beginning of the trading restrictions?
   - What steps did you take with your employees?
   - How did you communicate with employees?
   - Did you have to stand down staff?
   - How were they selected?
   - How did staff react?

Section 2. During the shut down

1. **Operations**

   - What activities needed to continue?
   - Who carried out this work?
   - How did you communicate with employees?

- Were the operating and social distancing restrictions clear to you?
- Were you clear on when and how restrictions would begin to be relaxed?
- What plans and preparations were made? How did you prepare staff for some resumption of activities?
- Did you get advice and assistance on the changes you had to make?

1. **Finance and Commercial**
   - How did you manage suppliers and creditors?
   - What issues arose with banks/financial institutions?
   - Were these able to be resolved satisfactorily?

2. **People**
   - What changes were made to the pay and conditions of employees? Did you qualify for and use JobKeeper?
   - How have you experienced working with the Federal and State assistance initiatives that have been put in place, like Job Keeper the BAS credit of $10,000? How did you find out about these schemes? Were these easy to understand?
   - What do you think about the JobKeeper scheme?
     ◦ Everyone gets $1500 regardless of the work they do?
     ◦ Did you change the normal duties of any employees?
   - What problems were you most concerned about?

Section 3. Resumption of some trading

1. When did you resume trading?
2. What activities were allowed at that stage?
3. What is allowed now?
4. How have you implemented social distancing?
5. What were the key changes you had to make to cope with the shut down and partial reopening?

6. How did you make those changes?
7. Did these work as planned?
8. Was fine tuning or major changes required as these were put into practice?
9. How have you coped with the reimposition of some restrictions in Victoria?

Section 4. Your reflections on management and leadership during this challenge

1. Up to now, what has been your greatest challenge?
2. What do you think has been done well?
3. What could have been done better?
4. How you sought feedback from your team/staff?
5. What are they saying?
6. What do you think they are saying or thinking?
7. Have or will you change the way things work here into the future?
8. What is your greatest concern about the future of the business?
9. How has your work as leader changed?

Attachment 2

Australian Hotels Association Covid–19 Resources

The Coronavirus crisis is creating extreme uncertainty for hotels. We will continue to provide relevant information to members to assist in the management of what is a very unpredictable situation.

We are working closely with Federal Government to obtain the most up-to-date advice. Because the situation is rapidly shifting, we have established this page to provide regular updates and advice as developments unfold.

For specific questions relating to your individual circumstances, please contact your State or Territory branch. Refer https://aha.org.au/covid-19-resources/ for Media Releases and other Resources & Information.

Notes

[1] Systems Leadership: Creating Positive Organisations. 2nd Edition. Ian Macdonald, Catherine Burke and Karl Stewart. Routledge 2018 pg 204

[2] Systems Leadership: Creating Positive Organisations. 2nd Edition. Ian Macdonald, Catherine Burke and Karl Stewart. Routledge 2018 pg 207

[3] Systems Leadership: Creating Positive Organisations. 2nd Edition. Ian Macdonald, Catherine Burke and Karl Stewart. Routledge 2018 pg 87

CONCLUSIONS

A wide cross section of organisations have been reviewed in the course of this study. They range from small businesses to global corporations operating in Australia, the United Kingdom, the Americas and beyond. The studies illustrate recurring themes whether the entity operates in public, private or not for profit sectors.

Looking at the studies as a whole, insights into wider community, economic and political leadership issues emerge, within and between countries. A key question arises in this context: are the principles and models of Systems Leadership (SL) applicable to the level of individual states within federal systems of government, such as Australia and at the level of the nation state?

In this concluding chapter, it is argued that using SL helps to understand the generally successful responses of the individual organisations studied but also the different outcomes observed at the state and national level. This does not mean SL is being applied by leaders in a conscious and deliberate way but the extent to which organisation and leadership responses in practice align with SL, helps identify leadership and organisational patterns practice which can be repeated in the future to promote effective organisations and social cohesion. The balance of this chapter seeks to apply the concepts discussed in the various organisational case studies to national and state governments.

General Application of Technical, Commercial and Social Domains (STC) of Work

In Chapter 9, for example, the concept of Domains of Work was used to describe three general areas evident in all organisations. The STC domains are of equal importance and an organisation cannot function effectively unless it is clear how the work is done in each domain and how it interacts with the two other interdependent domains. This concept is equally applicable to systems of government and to analysing government responses to the pandemic. The descriptions below of the STC domains at a governmental level illustrate this point in the context of Covid-19.

Technical

- The scientific and medical work that has gone on around the world to understand the virus and develop a vaccine.
- The research required to identify and understand different variants of the virus that have emerged including the notorious Delta variant.
- The work done to understand the modes of virus transmission essential for informing the design of many crucial systems to manage risks such as in hotel quarantine, hospitals, modes of transportation and the PPE required in these different environments.

Commercial

- Predicting and measuring the business and budgetary costs of suspension and lockdown of economic and commercial activity.
- The development and deployment of financial assistance programs to individuals and to business enterprises
- Public finance and borrowing initiatives to manage the longer term macro-economic issues arising.

Social (people)

- Communicating the public health measures and restrictions that people must observe and why, including to groups from diverse cultures and in homes where English is not the primary language.
- Explaining the reasons for changes over time and the basis for different requirements to be observed in different geographic areas or industrial sectors and occupations.
- Developing and implementing procedures for the enforcement of restrictions and public health standards.

Successful organisational responses to the pandemic described in this study demonstrate the need to integrate work across these three domains. The Education sector case study highlighted the need to fund, develop and deploy the technical capability to support a major shift to online learning. Online learning strategies which paid close attention to the individual learning needs of students, ensured access to the required computer equipment and supported teachers to do their work free from the usual demands of the education bureaucracy proved to be effective.

In the Newmont case study, when the commercial decision to suspend operations was made, the necessary technical measures were taken to ensure this was done safely and the global IT team helped get necessary equipment to employees at home. Employee support was focused on the holistic wellbeing of the workforce - physical, mental and financial. Employees continued to be paid and additional measures to assist local communities were taken. Operating losses were incurred in the short term, but the commercial and social domains of the work required were not seen as a trade-off. An integrated approach to all the STC systems involved allowed the organisation to emerge more resilient and socially cohesive.

This contrasts to government responses in countries frequently used to benchmark Australia. In the UK for example, Boris Johnson in a TV address to the nation on 22nd September 2020, announcing early closing for pubs, put the trade-off he saw in these terms:

If we were forced into a new national lockdown, that would threaten not just jobs and livelihoods but the loving human contact on which we all depend ... We must do all we can to avoid going down that road again.

This was part of a pattern of three general lockdowns followed by progressive easing of restrictions and then reimposition of general restrictions in response to the successive waves of the virus. The same pattern is evident in many countries including Germany, France, Canada, New Zealand and Australia. The table below illustrates the different outcomes between the USA, UK and Sweden, countries that eschewed restrictions on economic activity compared to Australia and New Zealand.

USA	United Kingdom	Sweden	Australia	New Zealand
191.28	197.21	142.61	3.86	0.53

Deaths per Thousand of Population August 2021. (Wikipedia, the free encyclopedia)

In Australia, the public health response and adherence to stringent lockdown measures minimised the transmission of the virus in the community. The result was that Australia was less hard hit economically than other countries. GDP was 2.4% lower in 2020 than in 2019, compared to the UK 4.4% and was far smaller than the average rate of - 4.7% across advanced economies. (https://www.austrade.gov.au/benchmark-report/resilient-economy)

Over the course of 2020 and 2021 however, rapid progress on the development and deployment of vaccines (technical domain) made the trade-off less stark, mitigating of the public health consequences (deaths and incidence of cases) associated with the opening up of economic activity. For instance, in the UK by mid-August this year, second dose vaccinations had reached 76.7% of the population over 16 years and the 7-day rolling average death rate had fallen to 0.9%. On this basis, the government can continue to support the opening up economic and social activity (commercial and social domains). Thus, the potential exists for the integration of government policy across the S T C domains of work but at the cost of many more lives compared to Australia. In Australia, where the rate of vaccination for the population is currently less than half of the UK, targets of at least 70% vaccination rates for the population have been set to avoid the need for periodic lockdowns to manage outbreaks of the highly infectious Delta variant of the virus. Different pathways have been followed across these domains and measures relevant to each will be required to evaluate which strategy proves the most effective, over the longer term.

Systems of equalisation and differentiation

Initial and ongoing responses to the pandemic can be analysed by reference to the SL concept of systems of differentiation, such as border closures and travel restrictions applying in particular areas or locations and systems of equalisation, whereby restrictions and lockdowns apply to everyone in a region or country. The purpose of both types of systems has been to prevent the spread of Covid-19 to that population.

Border closures, that is, preventing entry of potential sources of infection into a region or community has been a standard response for thousands of years. Usually, it is easily justified by the ruling authority as a necessary protection from outsiders that pose a risk to the safety and wellbeing of the community allegedly at risk. Justifying the basis of differentiation can be more difficult when it applies internally to a section of the community only –" why are people in that location or occupation allowed to go to work and we can't? We haven't had any cases of Covid-19 for 6 months!". It gets even more complex when the operating context of the system (whether of equalisation or differentiation) is quickly changing. This has been the case in Australia and elsewhere when authorities, needing to respond to successive waves and variants of the corona virus, have had to extend exclusion boundaries or change the basis of differentiation within a group on the basis of new epidemiological or clinical data. SL predicts that unless that unless the basis of differentiation or equalisation can be clearly explained and related to the purpose of the system it will be judged to be unfair.

In Chapter 9 the JobKeeper system was discussed; initially a system of equalisation for Australians unable to work because of the pandemic but still employed. Everyone received the same payment regardless of the type of job involved and the wages normally paid because of the skill and experience required. But as discovered, tensions quickly arose because employees on lower job classifications and sometimes with much less experience and time in the job, received the same payment as normally higher remunerated higher skilled jobs in the same business. Subsequent changes to the design of JobKeeper did provide for some differentiation to address this felt unfairness. Overall, the feedback on this policy has been overwhelmingly positive and in the context of further lockdowns, calls for reintroduction of the scheme are widespread.

As the pandemic persisted and the economic impact and budgetary costs for government escalated, scope for differentiation in systems of equalisation emerged. Politicians frequently described such changes as "more nuanced". Occupations and commercial activities exempted have been extensive ranging from doctors to undertakers, from bottle shops to courts and tribunals, post offices to financial institution, from supermarkets to the corner grocery store. Where the basis of differentiation has not been clearly explained or justified, sharp criticism quickly followed, especially if the community judged that special treatment was being afforded to the wealthy and the well connected. Nicole Kidman's exemption from travel restrictions in Hong Kong and Dominic Cummings car trip to Durham during lockdown and when infected with Covid 19 come to mind.

The early and decisive action by those leaders with the courage and judgment to quickly impose restrictions seems vindicated by the significantly lower levels of mortality in those countries. In the USA and the UK, in the early stages of the pandemic in 2020, it is arguable that the opposite approach was apparent. The threat to public health was seriously underestimated or in the case of the USA under President Trump was branded as "fake news". Business as usual prevailed with constraints on the community and business activity slow to be implemented and quite limited in scope.

The preceding discussion illustrates how these aspects of SL help explain the different outcomes of policy and system responses to the pandemic. It shows how the rational of equalisation or differentiation in the system must be clearly explained and communicated and related to what must be done to achieve the purpose of the system.

Tools of Leadership - Systems, Symbols and Behaviour

The case studies on the NHS and ICU in the UK have highlighted the negative consequences for an organisation and its people when organisation and leadership behaviours, systems and symbols are contradictory. The disconnect between symbolic behaviour, rhetoric and systems was exemplified by the government pay system, which after all the apparent adulation: "Protect the NHS...heroes going out to the frontline", offered a 1% pay rise in NHS. Many healthcare staff struggled with it and would have preferred a better way of being rewarded for going above and beyond in personal risks and effort and hours of work.

The Newmont case study provides a stark contrast. A purpose statement to help guide work across the global business was developed at the outset:

"To work together, in accordance with our values, to protect our people and business through this unprecedented crisis."

A set of guiding principles were set to support decision making around three key themes:

- The health, safety and wellbeing of its people and the community.
- Working together with local communities and host governments.
- Application of Newmont's business, leadership and operating models.

These principles guided operations, significant support to local communities financially and in kind and employee support, including income maintenance and programs to support employees and family wellbeing. During the phases of the pandemic, decision making was increasingly decentralised with clear roles and authorities. Success was recognised and lessons shared across the group. Leadership behaviour, systems and symbols were integrated and aligned. A more productive and cohesive organisation was the outcome. The CEO Tom Palmer described what he did as a "pragmatic approach". On closer examination the strategy developed bears a remarkable resemblance to what would be prescribed by the application of SLT. Perhaps it bears out Kurt Lewin's observation "there's nothing so practical as good theory", (Kurt Lewin 1951)

Towards Social Cohesion?

This concluding analysis has sought to demonstrate how the models and principles of SL applied to an individual organisation are just as applicable to government structures and organisations across entire countries. Case studies have highlighted the importance of social process analysis: the work to understand the mythologies of the community involved and to make predictions about how leadership behaviours, systems and symbols evident in actions to address the pandemic will be judged positively or negatively against universal human values - courage, fairness, honesty, respect for human dignity, love and trust.

Where this work was done well (explicitly or implicitly) such as in the preparation for online work in the Education and Courts System case studies, the outcomes were positive. This contrasts with the potentially divisive outcomes indicated in the NHS, ICU and South African studies.

It is also clear that the social process analysis necessary to maintain alignment across systems, symbols and leadership behaviours is invariable highly complex work when dealing with systems which must operate in a coherent and integrated way across the diverse economic and social structures that comprise a state or a nation. Merit based systems which encourage the progression capability to leadership positions in society are needed more than ever, especially in the public service. In this context, the increased number, power and influence of politically appointed advisers accountable only to the Minister, commonplace in Australia and the UK, is concerning.

In the face of the enduring nature of the pandemic, restrictions on social and economic activity

have continued. Unsurprisingly, resistance and opposition to these constraints on normal life have grown. The lack of certainty as to when restrictions can be eased or removed adds to social tensions. The rationale for starting or easing restrictions and for differentiation between social groups or geographic areas is not always clear and protests, not always peaceful, are occurring across many countries.

No country can claim great success in responding to the Covid-19 pandemic. It is possible to gain some insights into why some initiatives have worked better than others when looking at individual organisations. The purpose of these studies has been to show the systems and models of SL are relevant to understanding and seeking better outcomes whatever the scale and nature of the organisation.

A number of consultancies and individuals around the world have successfully built businesses applying to some extent the Systems Leadership (SL) concepts with client organisations. Many of these people and others who have developed a deep interest in SL came together to establish a formal interest group as a vehicle for further development of SL, its application and their understanding of both. This group has become the Systems Leadership Development Association (SLDA).

The purpose of the SLDA is to encourage the understanding of the sustainable application of Systems Leadership in diverse work environments.

For more details about membership and the operation of the SLDA visit https://www.sldassociation.com

* * *

CPSIA information can be obtained
at www.ICGtesting.com
Printed in the USA
BVHW041224281121
622695BV00001B/1